GATT ACCORD AND INDIA

A CRITICAL ANALYSIS OF RESULTS OF THE URUGUAY ROUND OF MULTILATERAL TRADE NEGOTIATIONS AND THEIR IMPLICATIONS FOR INDIA

Edited by
K.R. GUPTA
M.A., Ph.D.

ATLANTIC PUBLISHERS AND DISTRIBUTORS

Published by
ATLANTIC PUBLISHERS AND DISTRIBUTORS
B-2, Vishal Enclave, New Delhi-110 027
Phones 5413460, 5429987

Sales Office
4346/4C, Ansari Road, Darya Ganj,
New Delhi-110 002
Phones 3273880, 3285873
Fax 91-11-3285873
E-mail gupta.atlantc@Axcess.net.in

ISBN 81-7156-449-6

Typeset at
APD Computer Graphics, Delhi

Printed in India at
Mehra Offset Press, Delhi

Preface

The General Agreement on Tariffs and Trade (GATT) is a multilateral agreement which lays down policy and procedures for the conduct of international trade. It was concluded in 1947 with a view to reducing tariffs and formulating trade rules aimed mainly at protecting tariff concessions. Eight Rounds of tariff negotiations have been conducted under GATT. The eighth, namely 'Uruguay Round', was originally to be concluded in 1990 but had to be prolonged as there were sharp differences on issues like agriculture, textiles, intellectual property rights etc. Mr. Arthur Dunkel, the then Director General of GATT, prepared a document in 1991 which contained the results of negotiations agreed to and his own compromise proposals in areas where differences persisted. These draft proposals came to be known as the Dunkel Text. With a few modifications made in subsequent negotiations the Uruguay Round was concluded on the 15th December, 1993 and signed by 117 countries at the Ministerial Meeting held at Marrakesh (Marocco) during 12-15 April, 1994.

The book contains ten papers written by leading experts in the field of international trade. It examines in detail the various provisions of the new GATT Accord and their implications for India. The paper by Dr. T.P. Bhat briefly examines the impact of the Accord on Asia-Pacific economies.

It is hoped that the book would be found useful by the students of international trade, government executives concerned with the formulation and execution of trade policies, business community and the general reader.

The accompanying Volume contains the full text of the new GATT Accord.

I express my deep gratitude to all the contributors who have worked hard to write their papers.

New Delhi, 1994

K.R. GUPTA

Contents

Contents

GATT : THE INDIAN PARADIGM

JAMSHED A. SIDDIQUI*
Senior Assistant Secretary
PHD Chamber of Commerce and Industry

It was around mid-nineteenth century when David Ricardo enunciated that nations and people would have the greatest prosperity and global peace by adopting free trade. This ideology gained ground in the USA in early 1930s. In pursuance of the free trade thinking, the USA signed bilateral agreements with 29 countries with the prime objective of mutual tariff reduction. The idea of a liberalised trade regime continued, and to some extent expanded, after the end of the Second World War.

1.1 Genesis and Growth of Gatt

The Bretton Woods Conference of 1944 suggested institutional arrangements to undertake post-War reconstruction of the global economy. To promote monetary stability and provide resources to reconstruction needs, the Charters of World Bank and the International Monetary Fund (IMF) were established at the conference. The need for a comparable institution – the International Trade Organisation (ITO) – to oversee the liberalisation of world trade was also recognised at the conference. These multilateral institutions were mandated to fulfil development needs of individual countries in a non-partisan manner to prevent recurrence of economic chaos which characterised the inter-War period.

Originally envisaged as the first agreement to be negotiated under the proposed ITO, the General Agreement on Tariffs and Trade (GATT) was signed in 1947 at Geneva by 23 countries including India. At the time of its inception, the main objective of GATT was establishment of a world trading regime in which countries would gradually liberalise trade among themselves. Therefore, reduction of tariffs on trade in manufactures was adopted as a major goal for GATT.

The instrument through which ITO was planned to be established – the Havana Charter – came up for finalisation in 1948. However, the US Congress did not ratify its formal structure which was meant to govern world trade.

---

* (1) This paper was presented at the Seminar on "GATT Accord: India's Strategic Response" organised by the Indian Institute of Foreign Trade (IIFT), New Delhi.

(2) Opinions expressed in this paper are those of the author and do not necessarily reflect the views of PHDCCI or its Managing Committee.

Instead, it favoured an *ad-hoc* arrangement like GATT. Thus, the non-establishment of ITO led to the continuation of GATT.

Over the years, GATT has evolved as the only instrument that lays down a set of multilaterally agreed rules to govern international trade. It also functions as a multilateral forum for discussions and negotiations on trade policy issues through which attempts are made in making the trading environment more predictable and liberalised. By taking upon itself the task of settlement of trade disputes, GATT has emerged as an 'international court' in which governments can resolve trade disputes with other GATT members. GATT is, therefore, both a code of rules for international trade as well as a forum in which the contracting parties (as signatories to the treaty are called) can discuss and find solutions to their trade problems.

The MFN (Most Favoured Nation) clause is the essence of GATT through which contracting parties grant each other equality of treatment in order to ward off uncontrolled and arbitrary protectionism. 'Reciprocity' is the basis on which the signatories negotiate tariff reduction for promotion of liberalised trade. Contrary to the World Bank and IMF system of weighted voting, the decisions making process of GATT grants one vote to each signatory irrespective of geographical or economic size. However, voting rights of GATT differ according to subject under discussion – while some provisions of the Agreement can only be amended unanimously, other provisions can be changed by a two-third majority. But majority of the decisions during negotiations are made through consensus than voting.

The functioning and achievements of GATT have, however, been subjects of a polemical debate. Often referred as the 'rich nations club', GATT has been accused of ignoring the problems of developing countries. That every round of trade negotiations under GATT has witnessed an amendment in the US Trade Act has strengthened the perception that there exists a symbiotic relationship between the interests of developed countries and the objectives of GATT.

The Gottfried Haberler Committee reviewed the functioning of GATT trading system in 1958 and concluded that the developing countries were facing an iniquitous system. Unable to cope with the GATT-determined trading system, the developing countries started raising their trade and development problems at the United Nations (UN). This led to the establishment of the United Nations Conference on Trade and Development (UNCTAD) in 1964.

The First Secretary General of UNCTAD, Raul Prebisch echoed the developing countries' view that the GATT did not treat the problem of trade as a part of their development problem. In response to such critical observations,

GATT incorporated Article XXXVI in Part IV which legally recognised that countries at different stages of development need to be treated differently.

Despite several amendments, periodic but intense criticisms, and challenges posed to the concept of multilateralism, the membership of GATT has increased to 117 countries which together account for more than 90 per cent of world trade.

1.2 Political Economy of Uruguay Round

In order to liberalise global trade and to strengthen the multilateral trading system through the removal or reduction of tariff and non-tariff barriers, multilateral trade negotiations (or 'trade rounds') are periodically initiated to improve the framework of GATT rules and disciplines on identified issues. Eight multilateral trade negotiations have so far been conducted under the aegis of GATT. However, of all rounds, the eighth round has been the most contentious.

The Eighth Round of trade negotiations was launched through a Declaration at Punta del Este, Uruguay in September 1986 at a special Ministerial-level Session of GATT contracting parties. The Uruguay Round - as the eighth round of trade negotiations is commonly known – proved to be the most ambitious and complex trade negotiations under GATT because of the paradigm shift in its agenda.

The multi-dimensional paradigm shift in the substance and scope of GATT is broadly reflected in the following: The new issues of services, investment and intellectual property rights were included in the Uruguay Round for negotiations. Further, there were two sectors in the area of goods - that is, textiles and agriculture – which had received less attention in the past but were taken up for negotiations in the eighth round. And despite a diversity of negotiating issues, the Uruguay Round proposed an integrated dispute settlement mechanism for various areas. Moreover, it adopted a selective approach towards negotiating objectives in different areas. Sooner or later, an additional dimension of complexity was bound to be gradually added as the Punta del Este Declaration gave mandate for negotiations in as many as fifteen distinct areas.

The Uruguay Round also specified that negotiations on trade in goods and services would take place on two separate tracks. Further, for the first time in the history of GATT, the Uruguay Round adopted a "package approach" to the negotiations. The package approach, it was envisaged, would enable the participants to seek and secure advantages across a wide range of issues - concessions given in one area may bring in benefits in other area.

The agenda, approach and action plan of the Uruguay Round was drafted despite the reluctance of the developing countries. The idea and initiative for a new trade round negotiations, too, came from the developed countries. The hypothesis that GATT, and especially the Uruguay Round, would only benefit the developed countries started proving right the apprehensions of developing countries. Such apprehensions only prolonged and strengthened the debate and mistrust between developed and developing countries about the objectives of a multilateral institution.

The task for initiating the Eighth Round of trade negotiations started in early 1980s when major developed countries were witnessing severe recession. Political and institutional constraints prevented these economies from resorting to structural changes. It is, therefore, presumed that the recession-hit developed countries substituted domestic structural adjustment with multilateral means. The Uruguay Round did not only envisage its framework to deal with 'border issues' but expanded its rules that had an effect on domestic policies of contracting parties. This was the major factor which raised the issue of "threat to sovereignty" among the developing countries, and later lent a 'schizophrenic twist' to the negotiations.

An incisive analysis of the initiatives taken for launching the Uruguay Round, no doubt, evinces that the interests of developing countries were not taken into consideration – only compliance to desired objectives were expected from the developing countries. On their part, the developing countries initially took refuge in 'escapism' by not perceiving any interest of their own. Later, in absence of a cohesive voice and group of developing countries, the asymmetry in their temporary common approach became more visible. It is, therefore, more to the discredit of developing countries for failing to reiterate, consolidate and effectively convey their reservations on various issues of Uruguay Round. It would be a fallacy to outrightly condemn the richer nations for the malaise of the developing countries as concerns the Uruguay Round.

The inward-looking and centrally guided restrictive economic policies have had a 'growth-choking effect' on the economies of developing countries. In its quest for achieving social objectives, the control mechanism prescribed, and covertly protected, the inefficient segments of business and economy. Even agriculture, land use, natural resources and manpower could not be exploited and developed to the optimal potential. Such economic weaknesses surfaced, and were exploited, during negotiations of the magnitude of Uruguay Round.

The developed countries set the tune for imposing industrial, commercial and financial liberalisation on developing countries by arguing that the latter's state intervention and social policies are barriers to trade. The emphasis in the Uruguay Round, therefore, has been relatively less on reduction of barriers to trade in goods than on the enlargement of the coverage of issues and areas under GATT.

The new paradigm of Uruguay Round brought forth the gulf in perceptions of the developing and developed countries. Simultaneously, it created a wider chasm among the developed countries as well. The argumentative negotiations among the advanced economies related to the extent and degree of liberalisation in crucial sectors. As a result, the Eighth Round of trade negotiations could not be concluded by the end of 1990 – the period envisaged for completion of negotiations.

The Ministerial Meeting held in December 1990 at Brussels for concluding the negotiations failed to achieve its objective mainly due to discord among developed countries. To break the impasse, Mr. Arthur Dunkel, the then Director General of GATT, submitted a comprehensive document on 20 December, 1991 which contained results of the negotiations where agreement had been reached, and presented compromise proposals in areas where differences persisted. The perception of the package was to accommodate the interests of all GATT signatories. The Dunkel Draft's attempt at concluding Uruguay Round of negotiations, however, did not succeed. Instead, it led to an acrimonious debate on the proposals of the Draft.

The US tried to conclude the negotiations after it received the "fast track authority". (Fast track authority is a device through which the US Congress delegates its authority to the Administration to negotiate. The basis of the understanding is that the results of such negotiations would either be wholly accepted or wholly rejected by the Congress.) However, the fast track authority ended in December 1992 and attempts at concluding the Uruguay Round were suspended.

Prior to the G-7 Summit at Tokyo in July 1993, the US Administration received the fast track authority which was valid until 15 December, 1993. It implied that whatever the US Administration negotiates would have to be placed before the Congress for approval by 15 April, 1994. The urgency to finalise Uruguay Round by mid-December 1993, therefore, had more political connotations than economic necessity.

1.3 The Final Agreement and Indian Arguments

A major breakthrough towards conclusion of the Uruguay Round was the 'Blair House Agreement' in November 1992 which led to some rapprochement between US and the European Community (EC). Later, at the Tokyo G-7 Summit, an agreement was reached among the major players (the US, EC, Japan and Canada) on tariff reduction in some sectors. Finally, the most contentious chapter in the history of GATT – the Uruguay Round – was finalised at Geneva on 15 December, 1993. The debate on GATT and its aftermath, however, did not conclude – in fact, it intensified.

The dilemma of the developing countries has been the predicament of India during the Uruguay Round negotiations. Despite the initial reluctant position on almost every issue, India later started exuding optimism on the outcome of Final GATT Agreement. To some extent, India's oscillating position is perhaps understandable.

The economic ideology of India had a known tilt towards 'socialistic pattern of development, when the idea for launching eighth trade round was initiated in early 1980s. By the time the Uruguay Round was launched in 1986, the Rajiv Gandhi Government had started selective and cautious liberalisation of the economy. The period of debate on Dunkel Text (1991-92) was a period of precarious economic situation for India. When some semblance of consensus on GATT started emerging in mid-1993, Indian economy was showing an all-round improvement in its health due to the economic reforms programme initiated. The Uruguay Round was finalised when not only India itself but the world is considering it as the potential high growth economy. Thus, India's ideological shift and economic situation reflected in its attitude towards Uruguay Round.

The changing Indian stance, however, percolated to many levels of the society with various versions of interpretations. The lack of communication and true information about the impact of Uruguay Round only compounded the already complex issue. Each affected (and interested) group revealed its own analyses by concealing (or misleading) the correct perspective. As a result, even though the Government adopted a stand on the Final Agreement, the perceptions of other sections of the society have remained unchanged.

Various viewpoints have been expressed on the areas of concern in the Uruguay Round negotiations since its inception in 1986. These concerns were expressed in a more coherent manner after the Dunkel Text was submitted. The finalisation of the Agreement has only sharpened the focus of differences that have come to the fore in the wake of multilateral trading system.

Broadly, the main issues of concern for India revolve around Agriculture, Trade Related Intellectual Property Rights (TRIPs), the Multi-Fibre Arrangement (MFA) in textiles, Trade Related Investment Measures (TRIMs), the General Agreement on Trade in Services (GATS), and the Integrated Dispute Settlement Mechanism under GATT.

The degree of concern varies from indifference to rhetoric. While some provisions like discontinuance of public distribution system (PDS) or reduction in agricultural subsidy no longer apply to India, their continuance as a political issue is being ensured. Contrarily, critical issues like sanitary and phyto sanitary (SPS) measures, and technical barriers to trade (TBT) are either mentioned as a footnote or are being treated with fatal indifference. It would neither be an exaggeration nor a folly to mention that if the Uruguay Round tried to transpose every issue into tariff negotiations, Indian citizenry is transposing every economic issue into a political conflict.

The latent conflict and visible difference of opinion primarily arises from the manoeuvrability provided in the Final Agreement for establishment of a multilateral framework of principles and rules. It is being argued that the Agreement severely militates against several Indian laws. The apprehension is that GATT would have an adverse effect on India's sovereignty and development priorities. Such apprehensions – some genuine and many exaggerated – generated rudimentary forms of paranoia. Inconsistency in governmental attitude towards GATT exposed the political and economic vulnerability of Indian society.

The merits of multilateralism and benefits of Final Agreement, too, are more optimistic than warranted by the inherent weaknesses of the economy. The transitional costs arising out of the multilateral deal are being overlooked. The pusillanimous debate is, therefore, either confined to sectional interests or plain economism. In the process, it is the dualism in society that has come to the surface.

1.4 Coping with 'NeWTO'

The Final GATT Agreement has attracted unprecedented attention and diverse reactions. There are, however, no immediate gains or losses for India as a transitional period of ten years is provided for GATT contracting parties to adjust to the new realities of the emerging 'New World Trade Order'– in short, "NeWTO' (acronym mine). However, a broad analyses of the implications of GATT Agreement on a developing country like India indicate the urgency to realign our policies and priorities.

India's response to multilateralism has always been lukewarm. Despite embarking on the path of liberalisation, the concept of centralised management of economy survives in a reformed and refined form with most of its anomalies, intricacies and infirmities. As a result, the whole Indian economic policy has been undergoing an agonising reappraisal. Economic policy reforms have been initiated on the assumption that self-regulating markets can be relied upon to restore the Indian economy to a healthy international status. However, the supposedly bold and encouraging changes are proving to be lackadaisical, inconsistent and intermeshed.

To survive, and emerge strong, in the post-GATT multilateral trading arrangement, India will have to devise strategic policies which can transform threats into opportunities and weaknesses into strengths. It must be mentioned that yesterday's experiences and responses will be inadequate to cope with future problems and challenges. The task, no doubt, is enormous as the implications of the Final Agreement on India would be multi-dimensional and uneven across the sectors.

The GATT provisions in the area of agricultural subsidies are not applicable to India. However, care has to be taken that in future the level of Aggregate Measurement of Support (AMS) – the total of all subsidies – does not go beyond the GATT-specified 10 per cent limit. In case of agricultural exports, India has a competitive edge by virtue of its low price and quality. But India's potential to export would depend upon the dynamism of governmental policy towards agricultural exports as well as on the ability to meet the strict sanitary and phytosanitary standards meant for such exports.

To exploit the tremendous potential in horticulture and floriculture, considerable efforts are required in the areas of infrastructure, institutional and legal framework. Government must consider increasing the ceiling on land holdings for the purposes of increasing agricultural exports.

India has to provide protection to plant varieties either through patents or an 'effective' *sui generis* system or by any combination thereof. The flexibility to evolve its own *sui generis* system cannot be a justification for complacency. At the same time, safeguarding the plant breeders' rights (PBRs) has to be given priority. A lot would depend on how pragmatically and quickly the Government acts in this regard to make best use of the five years' transition period.

The Indian drug and pharmaceutical industry has grown and flourished under the protection of process patents instead of the internationally accepted product patents. Therefore, Indian patent laws have to be drastically overhauled at the earliest to align them with globally pervasive laws. In view of the proposed patent regime, Indian drug industry will have to invest considerably in research and development (R & D). The focus of R & D will have to be on new chemical molecules which can be used for treatment of diseases predominant in India due to its tropical climate such as malaria, cholera, etc.

Again, much would depend on the Government's drug policy. Although the DPCO (Drug Prices Control Order) may become more relevant in controlling the envisaged rise in drug prices, controls on drug industry's overall profitability will have to be liberalised to enable Indian companies to plough back profits into R & D activities. Therefore, DPCO will have to be made more flexible in its functioning. The Government may also consider establishing a separate and independent commission to monitor drug prices in future.

The quality of drugs – a problem arising primarily from drug manufacturing units in the small scale sector – has to be improved with due consideration to safety and health of consumers. It is a matter of concern that the public sector Hindustan Antibiotics Ltd. has been considered as the worst offender in supplying sub-standard drugs by the Food & Drug Administration. Government must, therefore, consider granting fiscal and non-fiscal incentives to drug industry to spur technological upgradation, and export of generic and indigenous products.

The GATT proposal to phase out MFA over a period of ten years may not prove outrightly beneficial to India. As the products for, and process of, integration is not automatic, the review of implementation of each stage of phase-out period by GATT may be adversely used by the developed countries. The period of transition, however, can be utilised for technological modernisation and quality upgradation by the Indian textile industry.

The future of the textile industry is blurred by certain other realistic factors – the emerging competitive advantage in the global market would also depend upon the advantages accruing to India's competitors in the South East Asian region. Although non-quota markets suffer from their small size and low buying power, India will have to tap non-quota markets for cotton textiles. The forty years of protectionist policies have rendered India's textile industry uncompetitive in world market. In order to benefit from the liberalised trade regime, the Government will have to reorient the complete textile policy.

To cope with NeWTO, India will also have to do restructuring in sectors other than in which it is affected. For instance, there should be an institutional change in the agricultural sector by implementing extensive land reforms. Similarly, emphasis has to be on upgradation of technology as so far we have concentrated on appropriate technology and not on latest technology. While industry will have to restructure itself, Government may consider setting up a Tariff Commission to monitor duty structure and dumping of goods. Moreover, science and industry as well as agriculture will have to function in closer concert than they have so far. Finally, for a vast multilateral exercise aimed at policy harmonisation, polity and ideology alignment is as much significant.

1.5 Governance after GATT

The Eighth Round of multilateral trade negotiations made the task of developing countries difficult. While still in its mid-way, the Uruguay Round witnessed a fundamental change in the geo-political and economic structure of the world. The withering away of a bipolar world left the developing countries in an ideological dilemma. Their approach towards internal conflict resolution reflected in the hesitant policy changes. Due to similar reasons, formulation and implementation of change is being prolonged on account of resistance put to it.

The necessity to change, however, persisted. During the last three years of Uruguay Round negotiations, the twelve-member European Community successfully, if not smoothly, created the Single European Market (SEM), and the US entered into a free trade agreement with Canada and Mexico to establish NAFTA. Moreover, the newly industrialised economies of South-East Asia emerged as the most dynamic region of the world. Besides, the marketisation and democratisation of Central and Eastern European countries facilitated the acceptance of GATT proposals by the developing countries including India.

The 117 GATT signatories together account for more than 90 per cent of the world trade. Countries which are not members of GATT are trying to enter into the multilateral institution. And those which are not vying for membership are numerically small, and even smaller in their economic clout. Thus, a wide acceptance and application of the provisions of Final Agreement can be questioned only at one's own peril. Even deviations from the now agreed rules cannot be expected because of the procedures governing the settlement of disputes.

An inherent anomaly that has surfaced after the Final GATT Agreement is that the treaty provides the flexibility of sorting out certain issues on a bilateral basis. Obviously, finalisation of issues on a bilateral basis is a mismatch for the spirit of multilateralism.

The realities of multilateralism require countries like India to change administrative and institutional arrangements for effective governance. Problems would arise if national legislations are not aligned to GATT provisions. Therefore, the operational difficulties in governance by developing countries like India for tackling systemic differences in national priorities and international requirements would be enormous. For instance, India will have to replace trade distorting policies with trade-oriented measures, and transparency in administration of policies would be required. However, it must be mentioned that such changes have not only been demanded by overseas investors but also by Indian entrepreneurs.

GATT bestows few rights and imposes many obligations. On the other hand, India has always obeyed international conventions and agreements, and has translated them into national laws. By the same logic, there is no reason why the spirit of multilateralism should not be adopted when India is attempting at becoming an international player. Surely enough, political alibis cannot defy economic realities.

Multilateralism is now a reality. The essence of multilateralism – trade reciprocity – would make governance after GATT difficult. The country has to develop a defence mechanism against bilateral arm twisting on issues like human rights, child labour, environment friendliness and other such potential non-tariff barriers. Therefore, policy reform on the trade front should be pursued with greater vigour and a strategic intent. Economic diplomacy will have to be strengthened so that in future India does not fight its battle only on its own. In the changed scenario, strict rules and self-policing would be to India's advantage.

1.6 Drift Towards Strategic Response

India's response during Uruguay Round negotiations were never adequate. Therefore, the acceptance of the Final Agreement raised the controversy regarding the wisdom of remaining a part of multilateral trading arrangement. As yet, we – as a nation – have not been able to arrive at a consensus in devising a strategic response to the GATT-induced NeWTO. Probably, it is not being realised that the cost of complacency would be higher than the disadvantages arising out of multilateralism.

Despite liberalisation of various policies and procedures, India has so far been unable to define its ability and direction to conduct international trade in the face of a highly competitive international business environment. The size and content of India's export basket has remained almost the same over the past four decades. As a result, with the signing of the Final Agreement, India has entered into a mapless labyrinth without a compass.

The process of liberalisation, too, has not brought about any meaningful change in the critical areas which are crucial for enhancing India's competitiveness in the world market. For instance, the liberal policies have been unsuccessful in raising the level of in-house R & D in Indian industry. Consequently, Indian industry continues to suffer from technological stagnation and obsolescence. In absence of viable incentives, and not easier imports, the R & D intensity (the per cent ratio of expenditure on R & D and sales) has declined from 1.1 per cent in 1980-81 to about 0.77 per cent in 1991-92. (During 1991-92, the R & D intensity of Korean industry was about 5 per cent). The lack of an effective National Technology Policy is reflected in the fact that even this small level of R & D activity is highly concentrated as only 5 per cent of the companies account for 50 per cent of the total R & D expenditure.

Similar drift in policy formulation is also visible in other areas as well. The eco-labelling scheme for environment-friendly products is yet to get a concrete shape. And the proposed National Quality Council, for monitoring ISO 9000 certifying agencies and their procedures, is long overdue. Further, an effective information system for initiating anti-dumping and countervailing investigations will have to be evolved and strengthened with an equal emphasis on strengthening of anti-dumping laws. Unless such changes are effectively implemented, there would be "Voluntary Investment Restraints" by overseas and local entrepreneurs.

Political maturity and unambiguous intentions are need of the hour. A case in point is intellectual property rights. While China has adopted product patents to derive benefits from the emerging multilateral trade regime, India is still debating on the merits and demerits of process and product patents. Although neither prior studies on determinants of foreign direct investment (FDI) nor the surveys on intellectual property right (IPR) provide any proportional relationship of FDI and IPR, yet the presence of strong IPR does have a bearing on FDI. The absence of a strong IPR would probably result in dominant role of trade rather than real FDI inflow.

The country has yet to respond strategically to the impending realities of multilateralism. Agriculture and skilled manpower has to be advantageously used. There has to be a substantial improvement in production and productivity. A viable welfare system for India's labour and changes in labour policies is still due. Quality of labour and products will have to get urgent priority. Consumer sovereignty and consumer protection is yet to get its due recognition. Moreover, a greater transparency in the tariff system is needed. It must be realised that delays in these areas would only mean gradual corrosion of the little gains that have been made in a liberalised regime.

In the emerging NeWTO, non-tariff barriers will have to be encountered. India should aim at discouraging their proliferation, if not blocking it for ever. Further, it is also anticipated that GATT-like trade initiatives would also be channelled through regional trading blocs. Therefore, there is no escapism from the realities of multilateralism. Instead, India must quickly take decisions based on its national interests so as to minimise the adverse effects and maximise the oppportunities arising out of GATT.

It is indeed a cause for concern that we have not been alert before events overtook us. Now, when perceptions have transformed into realities, a defeatist approach cannot adequately take care of the options available to the country. The lethargic pace of liberalisation has to be accelerated to our advantage lest the drift in evolving a strategic response turns into a national desperation.

1.7 Some Conclusions

At the end of multilateral negotiations of the magnitude of Uruguay Round, there are no outright winners or losers – that no country is fully contended with the outcome is a testimony to this fact. Contracting parties have to concede some ground in order to expand coverage in other areas, and this holds true for both developed and developing countries. Thus, there are those who win more and those who win less. The idea of "staying out" of GATT should, therefore, be abandoned. In view of the ongoing economic reforms process, India must accept the GATT Agreement for its own advantageous reasons.

In a truly democratic set up like ours, economic issues of the dimension of GATT have the tendency to drift into emotive arena of individuals and groups. As a result, there has been considerable debate on the issues of "threat to sovereignty" and "instrument of recolonisation". In the presence of such concentrically diversified viewpoints, issues of the nature of GATT are a matter of relative judgment. However, one point must be conceded to GATT – that it is a treaty based on the 'Doctrine of Free Consent'. To be a part of the treaty is a sovereign decision – it is not based on coercion or compulsion but on argument and persuasion.

Another related issue in this regard is whether it is advantageous to India to be a party to the multilateral trading arrangement of GATT. Numerous arguments may be, and are, forwarded for remaining out of the GATT-led trade regime. However, one reason that can be sighted in favour of remaining with GATT is the fact that it is the only forum internationally available which lays down the rules for conducting international trade. Non-participation in the GATT system would mean frequent bilateral negotiations with every country to secure MFN status which may result in conceding more than what would be conceded under GATT. Even the transaction cost involved in negotiating 28 separate bilateral agreements with 116 individual countries (a total of 3248 agreements) would be considerable.

The GATT system provides greater predictability to international trade and trends. Further, the mechanism provides multilateral constraints for any unilateral action. In the GATT forum, the developing countries can at least adopt a different stance on certain issues which is different from the extreme of unilateralism that is sometimes advocated by the developed countries. Therefore, a set of multilateral rules is preferable rather than no multilateral rules at all.

Opinion would, however, remain divided over the cost of staying out than being in the system. Some view the 'fear of isolation' and the 'benefits of multilateralism' as a myth and believe that isolating an economy of the size of India would imply some cost for the isolator too. Undoubtedly, the gains or losses would largely depend on how the multilateral trading system is practised by those who wield economic power and vision. It is estimated that India's exports would go up by $ 2 billion per annum as a result of the Final Agreement. This anticipated growth may prove to be sophisticated conjecture if benefits are not derived – rather, extracted – by India. On its part, the agenda of GATT should be so implemented that it is able to unite diverse nations spread across several continents, and not create rifts in coherent concerns.

At a time when regional trading blocs are becoming vibrant, the fear is that regional groups would be more favoured than the multilateral system.

The task of developing countries like India would be to dovetail its interests between the strongly polarised 'group economies'. It, however, remains to be seen that how would a country like India deal with strengthening regional trading blocs in a multilateral system. Pragmatism, rather than pessimism, would be the key success factor for availing available economic opportunities across the globe. In this context, the proposed SAARC Preferential Trade Agreement (SAPTA) should not remain an unclimbed summit. There might emerge an unavoidable need for a 'single tariff area' for South Asian markets. Moreover, the challenges of GATT regime are common to all countries of South Asia. India, being the biggest economy, should take the initiative in this direction.

That India could not derive the desired benefits and concessions from the Uruguay Round negotiations can be attributed to two reasons. Firstly, India made unsuccessful attempts at economic diplomacy – the support of many of the developing countries could not be mobilised for our genuine grievances. Secondly, and as a matter of fact, not much could be expected for a country whose share is one-two hundredth of world trade.

Thus, in order to integrate into an increasingly interdependent and highly competitive global market, India will have to shed its passivity and undergo a profound process of economic transformation. The process would, no doubt, involve some trade-offs in maintaining a social consensus in support of economic reforms. India will have to review the sequencing of basic reform measures such as stabilisation, structural change and private sector development.

We have to identify ways and means which can accelerate the process of transformation so that 'economic decline' can be avoided and effective participation in the global economy can be secured. The problems of India will now have to be analysed against the broad international political, security, trading and economic environment.

Therefore, the necessary institutional, legal, regulatory and financial conditions as well as the requirements for modernisation of infrastructure, communication systems, plant and equipment, and human resource development would require top priority in the economic agenda of the Government.

In the backdrop of ongoing economic reforms process, India must make assessments of what has been gained in these tumultuous years, and of equal importance, of what has been and is being lost, and at what cost.

New trends are emerging globally. Globalisation and competition is being pushed by actual events, national authorities and international organisations. Consequently, the inward-looking national frameworks are being transformed into international rules. In the new international business environment, man-made comparative and competitive advantages have become critically significant.

India should analyse the realities of markets and devise a sophisticated pragmatic strategy to adapt to the new requirements. Ideological dilemma should not get transformed into "Indo-pessimism" which would mean movement from economic crises to greater uncertainty.

REFERENCES

1. Arun Goyal, "No immediate gains or losses from GATT", *The Times of India*, 22 December, 1993.
2. Balraj Mehta, "India in GATT Round", *Financial Express*, 15 February, 1993.
3. Bibek Debroy, "Uruguay Round : Cake's there for the eating", *The Economic Times*, 27 December, 1993.
4. Deepak Nayyar, "Dunkel Text : An Assessment", *Mainstream*, 7 March, 1992.
5. GATT Secretariat : "Trade, the Uruguay Round and the Consumer", *CMIE*, Bombay, September, 1993.
6. "GATT and Uruguay Round : The Eleventh Hour", *Business Standard*, 13 December, 1993.
7. GATT Secretariat : *The Final Act Embodying the Results of the Uruguay Round of Multilateral Trade Negotiations*, Geneva, December, 1993.
8. "Liberalisation fails to boost R & D", *The Times of India*, 1 September, 1993.
9. M. Satish, "GATT Treaty may affect Bilateral Trade Disputes", *The Economic Times*, 17 December, 1993.
10. Ministry of Commerce: *The Uruguay Round of Multilateral Trade Negotiations – A Background Paper for Discussion*, Government of India, New Delhi, 1993.
11. Muchkund Dubey, "Political Economy of the Uruguay Round of Trade Negotiations", (Parts I, II and III), *Mainstream*, May-June 1992.
12. PHDCCI: *Recent GATT Negotiations : Implications for India,* PHD Chamber of Commerce and Industry, New Delhi, 15 January, 1994.
13. R. Ramachandran, "FDI and IPR", *The Economic Times*, 18 December, 1993.
14. Rajya Sabha: *Third Report – Draft Dunkel Proposals*, Rajya Sabha Secretariat, New Delhi, December 1993.
15. S. Vinayak, "GATT a Bad Deal for Indian Agro Exports", *The Observer of Business & Politics*, 23 December, 1993.
16. Suman Sahai, "GATT's gain is our loss", *The Times of India*, 26 December, 1993.
17. Surendra J. Patel, "GATT as an Instrument of Re-colonisation", *Mainstream*, 22 February, 1992.
18. "Uruguay Round of GATT and Developing Countries", *Monthly Commentary* (Indian Institute of Public Opinion), January, 1991.

GATT ACCORD : STRATEGIC MEASURES TO BE TAKEN TO MEET THE CHALLENGES OF NEW IPR REGIME : SOME SUGGESTIONS

PROF. S.K. JOSHI

Director General, CSIR
and Secretary,
Department of Scientific & Industrial Research

The Uruguay Round of negotiations of the General Agreement on Trade & Tariff (GATT) have come to a conclusion. The final agreement arrived at is to be signed by the concerned parties some time in April 1994. Notwithstanding the apprehensions of the developing countries, a new international regime on the protection of Intellectual Property Rights (IPR) is in the offing.

According to the agreement, the provisions relating to IPR will come into effect after one year from the date of entry into force of the agreement. In other words, the enforcement of the provisions will be from 1995. The agreement also provides for the delay of implementation of the provisions of the agreement for a further period of four years to the developing countries. The agreement also provides another additional period of five years for a developing country which currently does not provide product protection, to extend product protection to such areas. In short a developing country like India has a total period of 10 years from the date of coming into force of the agreement to modify its patent law and make it consistent with the provisions of the GATT agreement. Therefore the new IPR regime will come into force in India only in 2005.

The GATT agreement stipulates certain norms and standards in respect of IPR which mainly relate to national treatment, coverage of protection, term of patent and grant of compulsory licence. The objectives of these norms and standards are for promoting technological innovations and for the transfer and dissemination of technology to the mutual advantage of producers and users of technological knowledge; for social and economic welfare and to a balance of rights and obligations. The principles by which the objectives are to be achieved are (*i*) by formulating or amending the national laws and regulations, (*ii*) adopting measures necessary to protect public health and nutrition, and (*iii*) by promoting public interest in industries of vital importance to the socio-economic and technological development.

It is an accepted fact that strong IPR protection and its strict enforcement are very important for a country to attract foreign investment and flow of technology into the country. Taking the example of the Indo-US trade relations, the main constraint is the alleged deficiencies in the IPR regime in our country. There is a feeling that India does not recognise protection of intellectual property and that it permits piracy and other forms of theft. Consequently, US has been exercising pressures on India to amend her IPR laws, particularly the patent law. The main amendment required is in respect of allowing product protection in respect of drugs and pharmaceuticals. In this direction US declared India as a priority country under the Super 301 provisions of US Trade Act.

In the recent years, the Govt. of India has taken various measures to liberalise the economy so as to merge it with the global economy. Emphasis has also been given for increasing exports to strengthen our foreign exchange reserves. By agreeing to the new GATT accord, and consequently accepting the norms and standards stipulated in the agreement, the apprehensions voiced about India's attitude towards IPR is expected to be removed. This would clear the environment and pave the way for attracting foreign investments in India and enhance the flow of technology. This would also prevent India from remaining globally isolated.

The main apprehensions regarding the provisions of the agreement in respect of Trade Related Intellectual Property Rights (TRIPs) are regarding the extension of (*i*) the grant of product protection to all categories of inventions, including drugs and pharmaceuticals, and (*ii*) the area of protection to agriculture, particularly patenting of seeds and biotechnology.

There is a fear that grant of product protection for drugs and pharmaceuticals will hamper research work in the development of alternate processes for the manufacture of drugs which are currently being marketed. There is also a fear that the price of drugs will rise. There is no conclusive evidence to substantiate that the grant of product protection to drugs will enhance the prices of the drugs. According to the GATT accord, product protection will be allowed only for the new products which will be developed in future after the agreement has come into force. As indicated above, since India has a grace period of 10 years to bring the amended provisions of the patent law granting product patents in the areas of drugs and pharmaceuticals, there is also no strength in the apprehension of immediate enhancement of the prices of drugs, which are now in the market.

It is also important to note that when the patent law is amended to meet the requirements of the GATT agreement, it will not have retrospective effect; meaning thereby that the provisions of the amended law will come into effect only from the date of enforcement of the said law.

Under the above said circumstances it is open for anybody to develop alternate processes for those drugs and medicines currently being marketed as well as those which may come into the market during the transition period.

However, the GATT agreement provides for a pipe line protection during the transition period. According to this provision from the date of entry into force of the agreement, the countries, which do not currently grant product patents in the fields of pharmaceutical and agricultural chemicals should receive the patent applications seeking product protection in such areas when submitted. In such instances, exclusive marketing rights shall have to be given to the applicant for the products covered in the said application for a period of five years after obtaining market approval or until a patent is granted to the said application or rejected whichever period is shorter.

There may not be any difficulty in receiving the applications for patents seeking product protection during the transition period. But giving exclusive marketing rights for the product covered in such applications may lead to legal problems. This issue will have to be closely and carefully examined and appropriate measures arrived at, to counter the challenges based on this pipe line protection.

Another problem concerning patents is the consideration of importation of a patented product, particularly drugs, as working of the patent in the country which has granted the patent. This aspect has to be considered on a case to case basis. This is required because in certain cases the demand for a product, such as a drug, may not only be very little but also may be required rarely. Under the circumstances, it will not be profitable to set up a unit in India for the manufacture of such a drug and the patentee may prefer to import the drug. On the contrary in the case of a drug which is required in large quantities and very regularly, and if the patentee prefers to import such a drug instead of setting up an unit for the production of the drug in India, thereby creating scarcity and higher prices for the drug, then, the Govt. would have to interfere and grant compulsory licence to those parties who are willing and have the infrastructure and capability to manufacture the drug in India.

To counter this situation, appropriate measures such as mechanisms for strict price control and for the strict enforcement of the compulsory licensing provisions of the patent law would have to be established and strengthened.

As regards the enhancement of the area of protection, the agreement does not stipulate grant of patent protection to all categories of inventions in the field of biotechnology. It requires grant of patents for micro-organisms. However, a careful attention must be given to formulate suitable guidelines to indicate the specific categories of the micro-organisms for which patentability can be extended.

The agreement does not also stipulate grant of patent protection for seeds. Option is given to the countries concerned, to provide protection for plant varieties either by patents or by an effective *sui generis* system or any combination thereof. As explained above we have a transitional period to formulate a suitable *sui generis* system.

This transition period of 10 years will have to be fruitfully utilised to take appropriate measures to meet the challenges ahead of us. The problems connected with the IPR regime should be tackled in a realistic manner taking into account the requirements of the country, interests of our people and attracting foreign investments in our country. The drafting of the provisions of the patent law to meet the requirements of the agreement and that of the provisions of the *sui generis* system would have also to be done very carefully keeping in mind the interests of the country and the rights of the farmers and research scientists.

I propose that a National Committee may be constituted to look into these aspects in depth and formulate suitable guidelines which will be useful in drafting the appropriate provisions of the patent law and the *sui generis* system which will satisfy the commitments made in the GATT agreement and also meet the requirements of our country.

At present the knowledge about the various aspects of IPR particularly patents amongst the people in our country is very poor. There is also a dearth of adequate trained professionals in the field of IPR in our country. Since IPR is going to play an important role in post-GATT period there is an urgent need to educate and impart training to the scientists, research workers, R & D managers, entrepreneurs and those involved in taking policy decisions about all the aspects of IPR.

CSIR has taken the initiative in this direction by organising a series of workshop on IPR on a regional basis, for educating CSIR scientists. We are also organising a similar workshop for those outside the CSIR system, which is scheduled to be held in Bombay in April/May this year. These exercises would have to be intensified during the next few years at various parts of the country at regular intervals, so as to educate a wide spectrum of the people. The proposed Committee may also look into these and formulate suitable schemes for meeting the above requirements.

THE URUGUAY ROUND OF NEGOTIATIONS : A TORTUOUS JOURNEY FOR INDIA FROM PUNTA DEL ESTE TO MARRAKESH

S.K. BHATTACHARYA,

The Associated Chambers of Commerce and Industry of India

I

Introduction

After seven years of intense and procrastinatory deliberations on 14 contentious trade-related issues at Ministerial meetings, the Uruguay Round of multilateral trade negotiations, which started at Punta del Este, Uruguay in September 1986, had finally come through with the declaration of Peter Southerland, Director General, General Agreement on Tariffs and Trade (GATT) "I gavel the Uruguay round concluded" on 15 December 1993. There had been several ups and downs in the negotiations for last seven years and the world trading communities were hesitant about the prospect of this round. The major reasons for deadlock were the intricacies of the problems arising out of three new areas that included for the first time in the forum of multilateral trade negotiations, lack of consensus among the contracting parties in any contentious issue and belligerent attitude of the EC and the USA in question of agricultural subsidies being granted by the EC to its farmers under the Common Agricultural Programme (CAP) since mid-sixties.

After intense negotiations, earlier on 20 November 1992, an euphoric scenario had emerged after the United States and the European Community signed an agreement shelving their oilseed imbroglio which was commonly known as "Blair House Accord". The extracts of the accord were (i) 15 per cent EC agricultural lands devoted to oilseeds would be set aside in the first year, followed by 10 per cent in subsequent years, for which the US would withdraw its punitive tariffs on EC food and drink imports, (ii) the EC would curtail oilseeds production to only 5.178 million hectares to achieve a final production target of 8.5 to 9.7 mn. tonnes against a record production of 13 mn. tonnes in 1991. As a reciprocal measure the US would cut its soyabean and other cereal substitute exports to the EC, and (iii) the EC would reduce its subsidised agricultural exports by 21 per cent (the US had asked for 24 per cent) and reduce its internal price supports by 20 per cent and its export subsidies by 36 per cent.

The GATT negotiations which started through the Ministerial Declaration in Punta del Este, Uruguay, September 1986, was slated to be concluded at the Ministerial meeting in Brussels, 1990, but it failed to achieve success due to reasons mentioned above. In an attempt to bring the Uruguay round to a successful conclusion, Arthur Dunkel, the erstwhile Director General, GATT, offered a compromise package in December 1991 which was commonly known as "Dunkel's Draft". The contents of the Dunkel Draft were not new. Almost 80 per cent of the accords had been arrived at Brussels in December 1990. Compromise solutions were suggested in rest of the areas. The Final Act of the Uruguay round as engrossed by the contracting parties on 15 December 1993 was more or less along the lines of the provisions of Dunkel Draft. The 500-page bulky agreement will be formally signed in Marrakesh, Morocco in April 1994, after individual contracting parties present their final tariff reduction formulae in February 1994.

Final GATT Accord in December 1993

The "GATT Accord" is termed as "momentous and historic achievement" because of its unprecedented deliberations encompassing all areas of trade and investment ever attempted. The new agreement has paved the way for funneling US$ 200 billion to US$ 300 billion more a year through the increase in exports beyond 2005, *i.e.* more than 1 per cent of the world GNP (world GNP was around US$ 22.5 trillion in 1992). World trade (both exports and imports) was US$ 7.6 trillion in 1992, of which exports were of US $ 3740 bn. (merchandise US$ 3640 bn. and commercial services US$ 1000 bn.) and import was in order of US$ 3849 bn. Rate of growth of world exports was 9.2 per cent (*i.e.* 6.3 per cent in merchandise and 12 per cent in commercial services) in 1992 against -0.7 per cent in 1991, whereas world imports grew at 9.5 per cent rate in 1992 against 1.4 per cent in 1991.

Such spurt in world exports (after getting the Uruguay Round text implemented) is expected to have a positive effect on India's exports too. Presently India's share in world export is 0.5 per cent and in world imports it is 0.6 per cent. Under the *cetris paribus* assumption, only considering the market share, India's exports is to increase by US$ 1.5 bn. to US$ 2.0 bn. per year, which may basically emerge from the liberalisation of MFN tariffs in agriculture and textiles, etc.

A World Bank-OECD study entitled "Trade Liberalisation : What at Stake" by Ian Golden and Dominique Van Dar Mensbruggle estimates that annual gain that may accrue to India from trade liberalisation in the Uruguay Round could work out US$ 4.6 bn. by 2002 (based on 1992 US Dollars).

Currently 40 per cent of India's exports to the developed countries is duty-free; she has to pay duty only for 60 per cent of her exports, the average (weighted) of which is around 4 per cent. US$ 4.6 bn. gain in exports is based on the assumption of 30 per cent cut in all tariffs across the board *i.e.* both for agricultural and manufacturing goods. This estimate is simply the difference between India's real income based on existing trends till the year 2002 and its higher real income after the Uruguay round. It is to be mentioned that the gain for China will be US$ 37 bn. during the same period though it is not a member of the GATT.

India is still a quasi-controlled economy having strong administrative controls in a wide range of areas. Therefore, in the short-run, gains may be unimpressive, but certainly it will pick up in the long run as the reform process gathers momentum. India is expected to import wheat, coarse grain and vegetable oils, but export surplus exists in rice and sugar. In the livestock sector too, the country is expected to be a significant exporter. Except for livestock in all other areas India will have to suffer negative terms of trade because price of the agricultural commodities (exported) will fall and price will increase in the imported commodities. The livestock sector looks more promising because India has a significant surplus, particularly in dairy products. World price of livestock products increases under particular trade reforms. The overall terms of trade shook is positive 3.4 per cent.

As a result of tariffs cut as agreed upon in the final accord, urban income and employment are likely to fall and gains will be accumulated in the agricultural sector which translate into a total welfare gain of 0.2 per cent of total base GDP in the year 2002 or US$ 4.6 bn. per annum. Urban demand decreases because food prices move upwards. This upward movement of food prices leads to a substitution of food items to other items. The 30 per cent cut in tariffs in manufactured goods strengthens this tendency. Moreover, urban income also drops because of a rise in unemployment in the organised sector, and lower real wages which is basically rupee devaluation to counter cheaper imports.

According to the agreement on tariffs, the developed countries reduce tariffs on industrial goods by 38 per cent. Exporters of industrial goods will thus have an easy access to world markets. Estimated boost to world income from tariff reduction alone is about US$ 250 bn. of which 90 per cent is estimated to have come from agriculture and rest is from textiles and garments.

In the area of tariffs, India has made an offer of reducing basic duty by 30 per cent. This offer is applicable to items whose *ad valorem* ratio are above 25 per cent. The duty reduction is to be made over a period of 6 years and covers raw materials, intermediates and capital goods but excludes agricultural and petroleum products, fertilisers and some non-ferrous metals like copper and zinc. It is worthwhile to mention in this connection that this tariff reductions are in line of India's own reform process and are consistent with the recommendations of Chelliah Committee.

Trade in textiles and clothing have been guided by the Multifibre Arrangement (MFA) for the last 20 years which is likely to be dismantled on 31 December 2005. 51 per cent of the quota items will be phased out before 31 December and the rest will be removed on that particular date. Presently world trade in textiles (both textiles and garments) is around US$ 248 bn. (1992), expected to go up another US$ 25 bn. when the phasing out process will be over. Since India's share in world textile export was 2.4 per cent in 1992, which meant that her exports would be up by 0.6 bn. Though the final agreement in this area is consistent with India's demand, yet she has to wait until 2005 to get full benefit of the integration process. To India, the removal of quota is heavily backloaded.

In the final accord, there is a provision for setting up a Trade Policy Review Mechanism (TPRM) and also the Multilateral Trade Organisation (MTO). The MTO will administer the Integrated Dispute Settlement System as well as the TPRM. The MTO will also co-operate with the IMF, the World Bank and other affiliated multilateral agencies to achieve greater coherence in global economic policy making. Under the General Council of MTO, there will be a council for goods, a council for services and a council for TRIPs. Gradually MTO will be the successor of GATT.

The Article XVII of GATT pertains to state trading. The final accord strengthens disciplines and transparencies of the operation of State Trading Corporations (STCs). This is more prominent to Article XVIII B and the related 1979 Declaration on Trade Measures taken for Balance of Payment purpose. Under Article XVIII B developing countries can restrict imports through quota licensing on BOP ground. Developed countries argued that Article XVIII B was resorted to indiscriminately and concessions made by the developing countries in other areas could be negated by using such restriction. The final accord clearly says "contracting parties confirm their commitment to publicly announce, as soon as possible, time schedules for the removal of restrictive import measures taken for balance of payment purposes".

The greatest danger of multilateralism is the mushrooming growth of regional trading blocs. Article XXIV of GATT permits its members to form customs unions and regional blocs. Untill now 18 proposals to form regional trading blocs are pending with the Director General of GATT. In the wake of continuing recession in the developed countries, there has been a growing tendency of protèctionism visualised in the industrialised countries restricting the flow of cheaper imports from developing ones. In the light of such development, India should ponder joining any of the trade blocs to counter the growing menace of regionalism.

II
SALIENT FEATURES OF THE "FINAL ACCORD" AS APPLICABLE TO DIFFERENT SECTORS

(i) Agriculture

(a) Salient Features of the Final Act

Group of negotiations on agriculture was one of the major negotiating groups due to its immense importance to developing countries. Agricultural issue was the major bone of contention between USA and EC which stalled the progress of negotiations for more than 3 years. It was mainly due to the "Blair House Accord" concluded on 20 November 1992 the Uruguay Round was saved from the brink of collapse. The outcomes of the Final Accord on Agriculture are as follows :

- World agriculture price is expected to shoot up by 10 per cent after the GATT farm deal gets implemented though this may happen in spite of increase in productivity. The rise in price is partly responsible for scraping the dumping and subsidised food exports on world markets.
- Till now American and European markets were characterised by higher export subsidies in agriculture, which have depressed the world price in recent years, because current world prices equal production cost minus the average US and EC subsidies. The GATT deal stipulates 50 mn. tonnes less subsidised wheat flow in the world market from 1995 to 2000. As a consequence of the final agreement, wheat trade will be diverted from subsidised regime to the free-market system.
- Tariffs in the agricultural sector will be reduced substantially (*i.e.* one third of the current rate), but still there exists a lot of ambiguities regarding removal of non-tariff barriers (hereinafter NTBs), though it is clearly stated in the final draft that all NTBs will be converted into tariffs and will be reduced substantially with an object of removing it after a certain period.
- Most beneficiaries of the GATT's farm deal will be the Cairns Group of countries *viz*. Australia, New Zealand, Argentina, Chile, etc. which can produce more and enjoy wider access to previously closed markets. Australian estimated gain will be in the order of US$ 1 bn.
- The value of subsidised exports must be reduced over six years under the terms of the now infamous Blair House Accord by 36 per cent over the base period of 1988 and 1990. At the same time the quantity of these subsidised exports must be cut by 21 per cent. The base period

will either be 1986-90 or 1991-92 if exports are higher in that period.

- Besides, Europe has managed to preserve direct payments to farmers as compensation for falling prices. Although income support for farmers must be reduced by 20 per cent in developed countries, the European Union (EU) gained exception from some direct payments. This means farmers can still be paid for growing less and for structural adjustments which is an important part of the reform of common agricultural policy.
- Substitution of NTBs by tariffs will offer European farmers even greater protection than they enjoy now. Under the tariffication programme all NTBs will be converted into tariffs and the tariffs of the developed countries are to be reduced by 36 per cent over a period of six years and for developing countries this reduction will be 24 per cent and will be carried out over a 10 year period.
- The issue of tariffs on agricultural imports has recently exposed to great controversy in Japan, because it has imposed 700 per cent duty on its imports of certain varieties of rice. The QR regime in Japan is difficult to convert into monetary levy.
- Countries with closed farm markets will have to import at least 3 per cent of domestic consumption of rice, increasing to five per cent over a period of six years. Japan has to import 4 per cent of its rice consumption in 1995 rising to 8 per cent and in case of South Korea, the initial imports has to be 1 per cent rising to 3 per cent in 1999.
- Trade distorting support (*i.e.* subsidies) for farmers will be cut by 20 per cent over a period of 6 years for developed countries and 13.3 per cent for developing countries over a 10 year period.
- The final accord will help EC to increase income by US$ 30 bn. from agricultural sector alone and in case of Japan it amounts to US$ 22 bn. over a period of 10 year after 2005. Least developed countries will be losing around US$ 1.5 bn. due to increase in price after the removal of subsidies.
- A recent GATT study shows that consumers had to pay a staggering US$ 354 bn. in 1992 for government support for agriculture. Europe headed the list with highest consumer cost of US$ 160 bn. and in terms of per capita US$ 450. The US ranked the second with US$ 91 bn. or US$ 360 per capita. Japan was third in the queue with US$ 74 bn. or US$ 600 per capita. Total cost for 24 industrial countries in the OECD was a horrendous figure of US$ 354 bn., averaging US$ 440 per capita. Total agricultural subsidies provided to the farmers of the developed countries amounted to US$ 200 bn.

(b) Domestic Support Commitments in Agriculture

The domestic support reduction commitments of each member contained in Part IV of the schedule shall apply to all of its domestic support measures in favour of agricultural producers with the exception of domestic measures which are not subject to reduction in terms of the criteria set out in the Article 6 and in Annex 2 of the agreement. The commitments are expressed in terms of Total Aggregate Measurement of Supports (AMS), and "Annual and Final Bound Commitment Levels". A member shall be considered to be in compliance with its domestic support reduction commitments in any year in which its domestic support in favour of agricultural producers expressed in terms of current total AMS does not exceed the corresponding annual or final bound commitment level specified in Part IV of the Members' Schedule.

(c) Conditions under which AMS is exempted

(i) a member shall not be required to include in the calculation of current total AMS and shall not be required to reduce;

(ii) product specific domestic support which would otherwise be required to be included in a Members' calculation of its current AMS where such support does not exceed 5 per cent of that Members' total value of production of a basic product during the relevant year; and

(iii) non-product specific domestic support which would otherwise be required to be included in a Member's calculation of its current AMS where such support does not exceed 5 per cent of the value of that Member's total agricultural production.

For developing country members, the *de minimis* percentage shall be 10 per cent.

Direct payment under "production-limiting programmes" shall not be subject to the commitment to reduce domestic support in case :

(i) such payments are based on fixed area and yields, or

(ii) such payments are made on 85 per cent or less of the base level of production, or

(iii) livestock payments are made on a fixed number of heads.

The exemption from the reduction commitment for direct payments meeting the above criteria shall be reflected by the exclusion of its current total AMS. Regarding Export Subsidy Commitments, the following export subsidies are subject to reduction commitments in the Final Act :

– The provision by government or their agencies of direct subsidies, including payments in kind, to a farm, to an industry, to producers of an agricultural product, to a co-operative or other association of such producers, or to a marketing brand, contingent on export performance.

- The sale or disposal for exports by governments or their agencies of non-commercial stock of agricultural products at a price lower than the comparable price charged for the like products to buyers in the domestic markets.
- Payments for the export of an agricultural product that are financed by virtue of governmental action, whether or not a charge on the public account is involved, including payments that are financed from the proceeds of a levy imposed on the agricultural product concerned or on an agricultural product from which the exported product is derived.
- The provision of subsidies to reduce the cost for marketing of agricultural exports (other than widely available export promotion and advisory services) including handling upgrading and other processing costs, and the costs of international transport and freight.
- Internal transport and freight charges on export shipments, provided and mandated by government, on terms more favourable than domestic shipments.
- Subsidies on agricultural products contingent on their incorporation in exported products.

(d) Special and Differential Treatment

- In keeping with the recognition that differential and more favourable treatment for developing country members is an integral part of the negotiation, special and differential treatment in respect of commitments shall be provided as set out in the relevant provisions of the agreement and embodied in the schedules of concessions and commitments.
- Developing countries shall have the flexibility to implement the reduction commitment over a period upto 10 years. Least developed country members shall not be required to undertake reduction commitments.

(e) Domestic Support Programme in Agriculture : The Basis for Exemption from the Reduction Commitments

The present system in India of minimum support prices for procurement and administered prices for sale under the *Public Distribution System* (PDS) are exempted from the reductions commitments in the Uruguay Round on agriculture.

Government service programmes (which involve expenditures in relation to programme which provide services or benefits to agriculture and the rural community) that have been exempted from subsidy reduction commitments are listed as follows :

- Research including general research, research in connection with environmental programmes and research programmes relating to particular products.

– Pest and disease control including general and product specific pest and disease control measures, such as early warning system, quarantine and eradication.

– Training services including both general and specialist training facilities.

– Extension and advisory services including provision of means to facilitate transfer of information and results of research to producers and consumers.

– Inspection services including general inspection services and inspection of particular products for health and safety, grading or standardisation purposes.

– Marketing and promotion services including market information, advice and promotion relating to particular products, but excluding expenditure for unspecified purposes that could be used by sellers to reduce their selling price or confer a direct economic benefit to purchasers.

– Infrastructural services including electricity reticulation, roads and other means of transport, market and port facilities, water supply facilities, dams and drainage schemes and infrastructural works associated with environmental programmes. In all cases, the expenditure shall be directed to the provision or construction of capital works only, and shall exclude the subsidised provision of on-farm facilities other than for the restriction of generally available public utilities. It shall not include subsidies to import or operating costs, or preferential user charges.

(f) Public Stock Holding for Food Security

Apart from the mentioned government service programmes that have been exempted from subsidy reduction commitments Annex II of the agreement on agriculture also lists the basis for exemption also. Paragraph 3 of this Annex relates to *public stock holding for food security purposes*. In the final agreement this is defined as "expanding (or revenue foregone) in relation to the accumulation and holding of stocks of products which form an integral part of a food security programme identified in national legislation. This may include government aid to private storage of products as part of such a programme".

More elaborately, "the volume and accumulation of such stocks shall correspond to predetermined target related solely to food security. The process of stock accumulation and disposal shall be financially transparent. Food purchases by the government shall be made at current market prices and sales from food security stock shall be made at no less than the current domestic market price for the product and quality in question.

There is a footnote provided for this paragraph, which states that "government stockholding programmes for food security purposes in developing countries whose operation is transparent and conducted in accordance with officially published objective criteria or guidelines shall be considered to be in conformity with the provisions of this paragraph including programmes under which stocks of foodstuffs for food security purposes are acquired and released at administered prices, provided that this difference between the acquisition price and the external reference price is accounted for in the AMS".

(g) Domestic Food Aid

Regarding *Domestic Food Aid*, Paragraph 4 of the annex defines, "expenditure (a revenue foregone) in relation to the provision of domestic food aid to sections of the population in need. Eligibility to receive the food aid shall be subject to clearly defined criteria related to nutritional objectives. Such aid shall be in the form of direct provision of food to these concerned or the provision of means to allow eligible recipients to buy food either at market or at subsidised prices. Food purchases by the government shall be made at current market prices and the financing and administration of the aid shall be transparent".

There is another footnote that further qualifies the provision of public stock holding for foods security purposes (para 3) and domestic food aid (Para 4). It says "For the purpose of Para 3 and 4 of this annex, the provision of foodstuffs at subsidised prices with the objective of meeting food requirements of urban and rural poor in developing countries on a regular basis at reasonable prices shall be considered to be in conformity with the provisions of the Paragraph".

(h) Implications for India

- Due to subsidy reduction commitments as agreed upon in the Uruguay round, India will be able to export more in the enlarged global market. This is due to decline in prices for reduction in tariffs and agricultural subsidies.
- India basically gives two types of subsidies in agriculture. One is non-product specific and other is product specific. Non-product specific subsidies are given to seed, electricity, water, bank interest etc. which is around 5 per cent of the total product well below the limit of 10 per cent as prescribed by GATT. Product specific subsidies are given to 22 items of which subsidies given to 3 sectors *i.e.* sugarcane, tobacco and hand-picked groundnut exceed 10 per cent. In case of these three items, if India satisfies two criteria *i.e.* (i) per capita income is more than US$ 1000, and (ii) share of a particular product is 3.25, then she would be brought under punitive action.

- The farmers would not have to pay for their seeds, as they would be able to retain a part of their seeds for further use. Though internal exchange of seeds is possible but commercial exchange of patented seed is not permissible under the new accord.
- Indian Public Distribution System (PDS) will remain unaffected from the subsidy reduction commitments.
- Presently total amount of subsidy (both product specific and non-product specific) given to agriculture is about Rs. 11300 crore. According to Final Act, India is permitted to give subsidy upto Rs. 30,000 crore. Therefore, as the Commerce Minister has rightly pointed out that India is giving negative subsidy of Rs.18700 crore.
- According to the Ministry of Commerce, Plant Breeders' Right legislation would be evolved which will adequately protect the rights of the breeders' and it will also incorporate the provisions for protection of farmer's and researcher's rights.
- India does not have to accede to the market access commitment for the farm products. This is because of her balance of payment problems.
- Agriculture would be the fastest growing sector in the Post-Uruguay round world. This would open up India's opportunity for exports of wheat and sugar at a competitive price. As these are labour-intensive products, there is enough scope for welfare gain also.

(ii) Textiles

(a) Salient Features of the Final Act

- The "Final Accord" upholds the Dunkel Draft on trade in textiles by providing a four stage formula for integration of MFA with the GATT system over a 10 year period. Only 4 per cent of the total volume of imports prior to the agreement are likely to be integrated with the GATT just after the conclusion of the Uruguay round. Thereafter, the first stage would integrate 12 per cent with effect from January 1995. The second stage will release an additional 17 per cent from 1988 and yet another 18 per cent will be dismantled from January 2003. The balance 49 per cent will be integrated at the end of 10 years *i.e.* 31 December 2005.
- Presently international trade in textiles is around US$ 240 bn. a year. With some exceptions, cheap and mid-priced goods and commodities such as thread are today produced in South East Asia, the fringes of Europe and Latin America.
- Tariffs on textiles will be reduced over the period and will be phased out subsequently. Economies of higher tariff *i.e.* USA and Austria will continue to have higher tariffs than in Europe and East Asia.

- The Textile Monitoring Body will be the nodal agency to supervise the system.
- The Final Accord has agreed for the transition period of 10 years instead of US demand for 15 years.
- The Final Accord on trade in textile is same as of Dunkel's Final Act. But in the new agreement, emphasis was given on bilateral talks to settle our dispute that may arise during the implementation of this accord.
- The developed countries had been demanding 'reciprocity' in textiles trade by opening the textile markets of the developing countries for foreign competition. But their move was rejected by the Final Accord.
- The USA and the erstwhile Soviet Bloc economies stand to gain most from dismantling the quota over a next 10 year period. The expected gain for the USA (to the consumer) is US$ 22 bn. and Soviet Bloc countries is US$ 20 bn. Average rate of tariffs in USA is about 10-12 per cent, but it is 50 per cent in case of India.

(b) Benefits for India

- As a result of new GATT Accord on textiles, Indian exports of cotton garments will increase substantially in quantity as well as value terms. Currently the premium on ladies cotton blouse quota to the US is as high as Rs.120 per piece which is Rs.100 per piece as the normal export price.
- In case of synthetic fibres, India does not have much comparative advantage. Therefore, it is very much unlikely that our export in this area will increase very significantly in the ensuing years.
- After much arguments and counter-arguments just 24 hours before the conclusion of final agreement, India's negotiators in Geneva had finally resisted the US move to enter India's textile markets. This placates Americans with promises of duty reductions upto 40 per cent on items in the minor textile chapters (under the harmonised system) covering flax, coated or laminated and industrial fabrics. It is estimated that 6.5 per cent of our total textile imports will be affected by this tariff reduction.
- India has given commitment under the GATT Agreement to reduce the average import tariff levels on 17 textile products from the current 85 per cent to about 40 per cent. It will be carried out over a 10 year period. The product groups have fallen under 3 categories *viz.* (i) vegetable textile fibres; paper yarn and woven fabrics (HS Code 53), (ii) wadding, felt and non-woven, yarn, twine, cordage etc. (HS Code 56), and (iii) special woven fabrics; tufted textiles, textile fabrics, lace, tapestries etc. (HS Code 58).

- According to a recent study by GATT, India does not rank among the first 15 textile exporters which include China, Korea, Pakistan and Indonesia, though textiles accounted for some 15 per cent of total Indian exports in 1992. However, in garments (clothing), India took the 14th place with US$ 3.1 bn. of exports with 2.4 per cent share in world textiles exports in 1992.
- According to new accord, India's potential gain in textile trade will be the maximum. Average textile import of developed countries is around US $ 66 bn. of which US$ 33 bn. from developing countries. Since one-third of India's total exports consist of textiles only, it is expected that the accord will certainly increase its market share from the current level of 2.4 per cent to 4 per cent. In this area, India has competitive strength due to its low wage cost comparable to South Korea, Hong Kong, Taiwan and Malaysia.
- It is estimated that after the the completion of the integration process, world export of textiles may go up by US$ 24 bn. per year. Presently, India's share in the world's textile trade is 2.4 per cent which means additional exports worth of US$ 0.60 bn. will be generated. But the gains or losses depend on our competitive strength comparable to China, Taiwan and South Korea.
- GATT agreement on textiles has covered following items for the removal of MFA quota based on 2-digit level harmonised system. The items are silk, wool, fine/coarse animal hair, horse hair, yarn and fabrics, cotton, other vegetable textile fibres, paper yarn and woven fabrics, man-made filaments, man-made staple fibres, felt and non-woven wadding yarn, twine cordage, carpets and other textile floor coverings, special woven fabrics, tufted textile fabrics, lace, tapestries, impregnated coated, cover/laminated textile fabrics, knitted or crocheted fabrics, articles of apparel and clothing accessories, not knitted/crocheted, other made up textiles article and worn clothing.
- Many of the product categories mentioned above are not governed by the MFA which implies that the definition and coverage of textiles and clothing have been enlarged in the Uruguay round. About 40 per cent of this enlarged coverage is already liberalised in the sense of being outside quotas in the EC market. For the USA, the figure could be around 35 per cent. Since 40 per cent of this sector is already integrated with the GATT, EC does not have to do anything more in this regard upto 2002. Most of the liberalisation will appear in the period 2002-2005. Therefore, it is alleged by India that the phasing out process as finally agreed upon in the GATT is heavily backloaded.
- India virtually gains nothing out of this integration process at the initial years and she has to wait untill 31 January 2005 to get real benefits of the liberalisations applicable to textiles trade.

(iii) Subsidies and Anti-Dumping Measures

(a) Salient Features of the Final Act

The final agreement of GATT says that a subsidy shall be deemed to exist if

(a) there is a financial contribution by a government or any public body within the territory of a Member (hereinafter referred to as 'government') *i.e.* where

(i) government practice involves a direct transfer of funds (*e.g.* grants, loans and equity infusion), potential direct transfers of funds or liabilities (*e.g.* loan guarantees);

(ii) government revenue that is otherwise due, is foregone or not collected (*e.g.* fiscal incentives such as tax credits);

(iii) a government provides goods or services other than general infrastructure or purchasing goods;

(iv) a government makes payment to a funding mechanism, or entrusts or directs a private body to carry out one or more of the type of functions illustrated in (i) to (iii) above, which would normally be vested in the government and the practice, in no real sense, differs from practices normally followed by governments.

or

There is any form of income or price support in the sense of Article XVI of the GATT 1994.

or

(b) A benefit is thereby conferred.

The Final Agreement prohibits subsidies in certain areas *viz.*:

(i) The provision of direct subsidies to a firm or an industry contingent upon export performance.

(ii) The currency retention schemes or similar practices which involves a bonus on exports.

(iii) Internal transport and freight and charges on export shipment, provided or mandated by governments on terms more favourable than for domestic shipments.

(iv) The provision by governments or their agencies of imported or domestic products or services for the use in the production of exported goods, on terms or conditions more favourable than for use in the production of goods for domestic consumption.

(v) The full or partial exemption, remission or deferral specifically related to exports, of direct taxes or social welfare charges.

(vi) The allowance of special deductions directly related to export performance, over and above these granted to production for domestic consumption in the calculation of the base on which direct taxes are charged.

(vii) The exemption or remission in production and distribution of exported products, of indirect taxes in excess of these levied on the production and distribution of like products when sold for domestic consumption.

(viii) The provision by governments (or special institution controlled by governments) of export credit guarantee or insurance programme against increases in the cost of exported products or of exchange risk programme, at premium rates which are inadequate to cover the long-term operating costs and losses of the programme.

(ix) The grant by governments (for special institutions controlled by and/or acting under the authority of governments) of export credit at rate below these which they actually have to pay for the funds so employed ..... or the payment by them of all or part of the cost incurred by exporters or financial institutions in obtaining credits, in so far as they are used to secure a material advantage in the field of export credit term.

The following subsidies are considered as non-actionable under the Final Act of GATT

- Subsidies which are not specific, within the meaning of Paragraph 1 of Article 2.
- Subsidies which are specific within the meaning of Article 2 but which meet all of the conditions provided below.

Assistance for research activities conducted by firms or by higher education or research establishments on a contract basis with firms, if the assistance covers not more than 75 per cent of the costs of industrial research or 50 per cent of the cost of pre-emptive development activity and provided such assistance is limited exclusively to :

- Personal costs (researchers, technicians and other supporting staff employed exclusively in the research activity).

- Costs of instruments, equipments, land and buildings used exclusively and permanently (except when disposed of on a commercial basis) for the research activity.
- Cost of consultancy and equivalent services used exclusively for the research activity, including bought-in-research, technical knowledge, patents, etc.
- Additional overhead costs incurred directly as a result of the research activity.
- Other running costs (such as those materials, supplies and the like) incurred directly as a result of the research activity.

(b) Special and Differential Treatment

Under the *special and differential treatment,* extended to the developing countries, GATT final agreement prescribes that developing countries which have not attained a per capita income of US$ 1000 per annum are exempted from their blanket prohibition on export subsidies. India's per capita income was $ 310 per year in 1992, well below the prescribed limit of $ 1000 per annum. Therefore, India is exempted from the subsidy reduction commitments, subject to the fulfilment of another criteria *i.e.* market share.

Apart from per capita income criteria, India has to satisfy the market share criteria also to get rid of the subsidy commitments. GATT document clearly says that developing countries have to phase out subsidy programme where it has reached the export competitiveness. An exported item will be treated as competitive if it attains 3.25 per cent share in world trade of that particular product for two consecutive calendar years. Developing countries that have attained a per capita income of $ 1000 and are export competitive in a product have to phase out export subsidies on that product within two years from 1995. Those that have not attained the benchmark of $ 1000 have eight years from 1995. The surveillance of this is not automatic but is to be channeled through the Committee on Subsidies and Countervailing Measures (SCM).

Another condition of getting exempted from the subsidy reduction commitment is that if the volume of subsidised import is less than 4 per cent of the total imports from any particular country having income less than $ 1000 per annum. The GATT accord on countervailing duty is applicable on the imports from developing countries, if the total import of the products from the developing countries exceed 9 per cent.

In case of India, this subsidy reduction programme does not hold good because its per capita income is less than $1000 per annum, and second, barring few items, its market share is less than 3.25 per cent. If we consider the individual items, only in case of diamond and diamond jewellery her market share is more than 10 per cent. Market shares of some major export items from India are diamonds (7.5 per cent), imitative jewellery (2.4 per cent), precious and semi-precious stones (2.4 per cent), synthetic organic dyes (1.8 per cent), essential oils (2.5 per cent), spinning machinery (3.0 per cent), garments (2.4 per cent), textiles (2.2 per cent).

(c) Anti-Dumping Duties

The Final Act of GATT has set several transparent rules on anti-dumping and anti-circumvention rules. Some of the salient features of the new agreement on anti-dumping duties are as follows :

— The new anti-dumping agreement provides for better clarity and more detailed rules for deciding whether a product is dumped. The accord also provides transparent guidelines for deciding whether injury is caused and the procedures for anti-dumping investigations.

— It sets rules on how long anti-dumping action can remain in force.

— On deciding whether a product is dumped, the agreement sets new rules for comparing the normal price of a product with the export price and it aims to curb the practices of arbitarily creating or inflating dumping margins.

— Due to new and transparent procedures, it will be easier for interested parties to present evidence in investigations. Preliminary and final findings in anti-dumping actions will be notified to interested parties promptly and in details. This was an answer to a criticism that GATT panels till now were too secretive to reveal as to how the agreement was reached.

— Labour unions as well as companies will be able to bring complaints to the attention of governments.

— Investigations on dumping will be terminated immediately if the dumping margin is found to *de minimum* (defined as less than 2 per cent of the export price of the product). If the volume of dumped good is negligible – generally when the volume of dumped goods from an individual country account for less than 3 per cent of the imports of the products in question, the same rule would apply.

— GATT panels are established in order to examine the results of dumping investigations but would not be allowed to re-examine the facts of the case. Though the US was vehemently opposing to this provision, GATT did not succumb to US point of view. As per the final agreement GATT permits only upto the stage as to how the case was handled.

— Demands for stricter anti-circumvention rules have been rejected and that the "sunset" clauses forcing a dumping duty to expire after a certain number of years would be protected.

— The US will no longer be able to retain dumping duties indefinately, over 10 per cent of US dumping duties have been in existence more than 20 years.

- This is the first agreed text ever achieved in the area of anti-dumping duties. Every previous deal had been imposed on countries with unreconciled disagreements.
- The volume of dumped imports is to be treated as negligible if the volume of imports from a particular country works out to less than 1 per cent of the market of similar product in the importing country. Indian exporters of steel ropes, wires and rods, which have been the target of US anti-dumping authorities in the past, may benefit from the new dispensations.
- Rules on anti-dumping duties will be clarified. Washington won its battle with Japan over keeping tough US anti-dumping laws but the treaty would require automatic scraping of sanction after 5 years.

(iv) Tariffs

(a) Salient Features

India is one of the major beneficiaries of the tariff reduction package as agreed upon in the Final Agreement. India's exports are not effectively constrained by the existing tariff levels of the developed countries which is already very low. 40 per cent of our total exports is duty free, and the average (weighted) rate of duty for the rest 60 per cent of our exports ranges 4-5 per cent. However, tariff rate is very high in MFA items *i.e.* textiles and clothing.

In the Tokyo round of negotiations, developed countries agreed to reduce 60 per cent tariffs and in the Uruguay round they offered to cut 40 per cent of the average tariffs. But finally, the developed contracting parties agreed to reduce tariff 38 per cent on industrial goods and 30 per cent on agricultural goods. All non-tariff barriers are to be converted into tariffs under the "tariffication programme" which has to be reduced by 36 per cent by the developed countries over a period of 6 years and 24 per cent by the developing countries over a period of 10 years.

(b) India's Offer in Area of Tariffs and Expected Gains

In the Uruguay Round of negotiations, India has already made an offer to reduce basic duty by 30 per cent, which is applicable only on items on which duties are above 25 per cent *ad valorem*. This duty reduction is to be made over a period of 6 years covering raw materials, intermediates and capital goods, but excludes agricultural products, petroleum products, fertilisers and some non-ferrous metals like copper and zinc.

In a unilateral measure, as a part of the current reform process which initiated in July 1991, India has already brought down its duty level to 40 per cent in the short run and 20 per cent in the medium term. In case of capital good imports, even this is reduced to 10-15 per cent under certain conditions. Indian government has already pledged to reduce import weighted tariff level from present 47 per cent in 1993-94 per cent to 25 per cent in next three years. Nevertheless, it has also announced that peak level tariff will be reduced from 85 per cent to 50 per cent in 1996-97. India has to reduce import tariffs on non-agricultural consumer goods to a maximum of 40 per cent and further to 25 per cent where tariffs are already below 40 per cent.

It is estimated that as a result of new accord, India's integrated steel producers will gain much as she is competitive in semi-finished products like billets, blooms, plates, HR coils and CR coils. Our export price of plate is approximately Rs.11000/ton, whereas international price is Rs.12000/ton, our export price of HR coil is $ 250/ton and international price is $ 270/ton. India's competitiveness in these areas will be sharpened by the Final agreement of GATT, where duties are proposed to be scraped from items like steel, pharmaceuticals, furniture and paper etc.

(v) Services

India has won a major battle in the Uruguay Round keeping banking, insurance and basic telecommunication sectors outside of the final agreement. India's banking and insurance sectors are monopolised by the government not even open the private service providers. India is extremely reluctant to open these sectors to foreign companies in the near future. The services provided by these sectors are to cater to the need of our development programmes which government does not like to jeopardise.

Another success in area of services is GATT's approval for temporary movement of skilled personnel to the developed countries. Right from the beginning India had been demanding for relaxation of restrictions on service operators to move in some categories of skilled personnel to a range of labour intensive services in key targetted markets. On average 10,000 Indian software personnel move to USA, EC and Canada each year. If we assure that they would remit at least $ 1000 every month then the estimated flow of foreign exchange will be $ 120 mn. per year. This is a major success for Indian negotiators in the area of services.

(vi) Trade Related Intellectual Property Rights (TRIPs)

(a) Basic Features

TRIPs was the most sensitive, complex and controversial issue in the Uruguay Round of Negotiations from the developing countries' point of view. New TRIPs agreement has far reaching impact on Indian economy.

For the first time it was included in the multilateral forum. The new GATT accord maintains *status quo* in the TRIPs agreement as proposed in the Dunkel's Final Act. TRIPs mainly covers seven areas *viz.* (i) patents, (ii) copyrights, (iii) layout and designs, (iv) trade marks, (v) geographical indication, (vi) trade secret and (vii) integrated circuit. Of these seven areas, all but patents are consistent with international standards and even in some cases Indian rules are better comparable to international norms.

India's Patent Act of 1970 covers almost 80 per cent of our patented products. Out of total of 5446 patents filed in 1969, 4158 were held by the foreigners. It declined over the years and finally reduced to 3765 in 1991 of which 2538 were held by the foreigners. During the same year 1491 patents were granted of which majority were held by the foreigners. This is less than 1 per cent of those filed in Japan. In the corresponding year patents granted to China were 3 times more than that of India. In 1990-91 only 87 patents were granted to drugs industry including foreign ones.

Our R&D expenditure is at such a low level and low standard that hardly any patent could be commercially exploited. It is estimated that the average R&D expenditure of private industry ranges from 0.1 per cent to 1 per cent of turnover as against 8-10 per cent as their counterparts abroad. Almost all of our R&D expenditures are borne by public sectors. Presently India is having 130 research centres of excellence and 300 engineering colleges, but we have yet to develop patents of significance that could boost our research morale.

(b) Implications of GATT's Final Act on Indian Patent System

Regarding Plant Breeders' Right, the Final Accord prescribes intellectual property protection for plants as in the following way, "However, parties shall provide for the protection of plant varieties either by patents or by effective *sui generis* system or by combination thereof". American submission to GATT was to demand protection for plants and life form exclusively through patents but this move was resisted by the European counterpart.

Europe submitted the choice of protection by a *sui generis* system. This was for two reasons *viz.* (i) Europeans have traditionally shied away from imposing monopolies on food which patents undoubtedly would do. They are exercised about the ethical dimension to granting ownership of life through patents. (ii) The other reason for inclusion the *sui generis* form was that the European Patent Convention (Article 536) itself does not allow the patenting of plants and animals and Europe, therefore, could not for its own reasons accept patents in this area. However, Europe did have an existing *sui generis* system of protecting plant varieties which is known as Plant Breeders' Rights (PBRs).

The *sui generis* form of Protection has been codified since 1961 in a body called UPOV a French acronym for an organisation whose English name is Union for the Protection of Plant varieties. The UPOV treaty was amended in 1972, 1978 and 1991. Prior to 1991, the amendment dealt basically institutional matters like defining plant varieties, conditions of membership and running the council and financial matters. The 1991 amendment introduced a change in the system and brought the existing system closer to patents. It also extended duration of protection offered to the breeders from the earlier 15 years for plant and 18 years from trees and vines, to 20 years for plant varieties and 25 years for trees and vines as per the 1991 amendment.

The new (1991) amendment radically changed the character of PBRs as a form of limited protection dealing with the exceptions granted to farmers and other plant breeders in using varieties protected by the PBRs. Termed as Farmers' and Breeders' Exemption these two very important exceptions allowed a PBR holders to derive benefit from his variety through seed sales without allowing him/her to monopolise the variety. The revised PBRs have abolished these exemptions. The US committed to stronger protection for life form (its own laws allow patents on plants and animals) played a key role in tightening up PBRs at the 1991 revisions.

Because of the Breeders Exemption, the pre-1991 PBRs allowed any plant breeder free access to a protected variety to use for breeding other varieties. The Farmers' Exemption gave the farmer complete rights over the protected variety once he had bought it. He had the right to save seed from his harvest to sow the next crop *i.e.* he could produce seed for himself.

After the 1991 revision, the Breeders' Exemption has been done away with. This means breeders will have to pay royalty to the PBRs holder to use his variety for breeding other varieties. The Farmers' Exemption on the other hand has been made optional.

The 1991 UPOV Treaty slates in Article 15.

"Each contracting party may within reasonable limits and subject to the safeguarding of the legitimate interests of the breeder, restricts the breeders' right in relation to any variety in order to permit farmers to use for propagating purposes on their own holdings, the product of the harvest which they have obtained by planting on their own holdings, the protecting variety."

At least one aspect is clear under the condition of *sui generis* protection given to Plant Breeders' rights, the farmers right to save seed is not free any more, it will come with a price tag.

Regarding Breeders' Rights, Mr. Peter Southerland, DG for GATT, made it clear that India would be perfectly free in protecting the traditional farmers' rights such as use of seed for planting for the next crop and for carrying out "across the fence" exchanges of improved seeds on non-commercial basis. Likewise it can provide for researchers to use improved seeds for carrying out further research.

Indian government has decided to constitute a group of scientists to evolve a new Plant Breeders' Legislation, which could provide rights to the breeders for a reasonable period of time, while simultaneously protecting the privileges of farmers and researchers. Government has not yet decided whether it will stick to UPOV 1961 or UPOV 1991. UPOV 1961 is more flexible than the latter. But if it does not have any option but to support 1991 provision then nobody knows what would happen.

(c) Drug and Pharmaceuticals

Drugs and pharmaceuticals is the major area of concern to India. India is having the process patents in drugs, pharmaceuticals, chemicals and processed food industries. GATT final accord says that India has to give product patent in these areas after 10 years. Drug producers in India have expressed apprehension that if the product patent is finally granted in this sector, prices of drugs would shot up immediately and the unbridled growth of prices cannot be checked with the existing machineries.

As against this apprehension, government has stated that the operation of Drug Price Control Order (DPCO) would act as a check on the prices of drugs. There is also a provision for grant of compulsory licensing for public non-commercial use. Government's explanation in this matter has been corroborated in the Director General of GATT during his recent visit to India. The stringent condition attached to the compulsory licensing in TRIPs agreement do not apply in case of public non-commercial use of patented drugs. If a government decides to grant a compulsory licence for the local production of an essential life saving drug for free distribution through the public hospital system, the country is free to do so without taking any consent from the patent holder. Many developing countries, are therefore, thinking of addressing concerns regarding the public use of patent monopoly through incorporating suitable legislations on restrictive business practices. Other features of the Final Accord on Patents are described below :

- There is a growing apprehension that drug prices will rise exorbitantly after the introduction of new patent regime. But this apprehension is not supported by the fact that 85 per cent of the drugs now in the market will be off-patent when new patent regime will come into force. Presently out of 250 essential drugs (as listed by WHO), only 10-15 per cent are on-patent. Out of 28 major patented drugs which cover

80 per cent of our total drug production, 22 become off-patent and genesic *i.e.* patent period of these drugs already expired. Only 6 drugs are on-patent which will be expired much before 2005.

— It is expected that every year 6-8 new drugs will come into markets that are basically in areas of AIDS, cancer, heart disease etc. and will be under patent protection. Even if prices of these drugs would be a little higher, government will have the right to grant compulsory licences to produce these drugs in the domestic markets at reasonable terms and conditions of the patent holders. Therefore, enough cheaper varieties of alternative drugs will be available in the market.

— Between 1983 and 1992, 400 new drugs entered the world market, of which 50 were antibiotics and less than 10 per cent of these drugs entered in India. Out of 250 essential drugs (as per WHO's list), only seven are currently under patents.

— The import of drugs under nominal tariffs, and judicious use of compulsory licensing provision by the Patent-granting country are permitted under the new accord.

— Good IPR protection and protecting public interest are not incompatible. According to the provision of the new accord, Indian drug manufacturers are free to "copy" upto 1988. It is only after 2002, that we have to set in motion a product patent system.

— In medicine, future discoveries are more likely to be in biotechnology rather than synthetic drugs. However, if a vaccine is developed for AIDS or some other diseases, we have the compulsory licensing provisions and the drugs price control mechanism (*i.e.* DPCO) to protect the public interest properly.

— Government would give "reasonable protection" to the plant breeders who develop new plant varieties under the agreement. Rights of farmers and researchers will be fully protected under the new GATT Accord. The proposed "*sui generis*" legislation would safeguard the interest of farmers.

— The agreement does not want patenting "naturally occurring genes" and "gene sequences". This move is consistent with the long standing demand of India.

— There is a provision in the final accord that under certain circumstances, government can undertake compulsory licensing for non-commercial public use as well as to prevent situation of either inadequate availability or exorbitant prices.

— The pipe-line protection clause (providing for exclusive marketing rights for five years for a new product patented in another country) would be in force five years before the introduction of product patent system.

III

MARRAKESH AGREEMENT : FINAL RATIFICATION OF THE URUGUAY ROUND OF MULTILATERAL TRADE NEGOTIATIONS

The tortuous and tumultous journey which started seven and half-years back at Punta del Este, Uruguay, culminated at the Marrakesh, Morrocco, through the ratification of GATT Accord on multilateral trade by ministers from 124 countries. The results amounted to 500 pages of comprehensive legal text (*i.e.* Final Act Embodying the Results of the Uruguay Round of Multilateral Trade Negotiations) and around 26000 pages (weighing more than 175 kg) of individual concessions on market access for goods and services. Experts have estimated that total income gains after the Final Act gets implemented will be in order of $ 235 bn. annually, and trade gains of $ 755 bn. annually by 2005 which will increase further, if service sectors are included.

A provisional estimate on the probable gains of the Uruguay Round Agreement shows that benefits are mainly concentrated on following areas;

— increase in market access security through higher tariff bindings 100 per cent security for agricultural products;

— 100 per cent security for industrial products entering developed countries,

— a 38 per cent cut in developed countries tariff on industrial products from 6.3 per cent to 3.9 per cent;

— a jump from 20 per cent to 43 per cent value of imports of developed countries will be given duty free treatment.

Out of 124 nations, 94 nations signed the final act of the Uruguay Round, 80 of whom have also signed the WTO. Morrocco, Guinea Bissau and Qatar have signed both the Final Act and the WTO. Rest will sign at Geneva. US, Japan and few other countries have not signed the agreement setting up the World Trade Organisation due to domestic legal requirements. The Marrakesh Agreement has reached into broad consensus that signatories will initiate concerted efforts to improve world trade and will be debarred from taking any retaliatory measure till the establishment of the WTO in January 1995. WTO is supposed to take full shape between January and July of 1995. January 1995 has been earmarked for the date of replacement of GATT by the WTO, which will oversee a comprehensive set of rules and disciplines covering every aspect of world trade including trade in services and intellectual property rights.

The Marrakesh Meeting concluded with six major declarations *viz.*

(i) Decision on the establishment of the preparatory committee for the World Trade Organisation (WTO)

(ii) Decision on the acceptance and accession to the agreement establishing the WTO.

(iii) Decision on trade and environment.

(iv) Decision on trade in services and the environment.

(v) Decision on organisation and financial consequences following from the implementation of the agreement establishing the WTO.

(vi) The Marrakesh Declaration.

In Marrakesh all contracting parties to GATT were basically divided into two groups on issue of "Social Clause", USA had been vigorously trying to include "Social Clause" in the agenda of the preparatory committee of the WTO. In a rare gesture of collusion between USA and France on any contentious issue in the history of Uruguay Round of negotiations, both of them, for the first time, were unanimous for the inclusion of the "Social Issue" in the final agreement of GATT in Marrakesh. They emphatically said that the protection of labour rights should be put at the top of the agenda. The intention behind such move was to hit the export-oriented developing countries with trade sanctions on the ground that these countries have been capturing markets of the developed ones by using the cheap labours which they used to have historically. USA wanted the preparatory committee of the WTO which would replace GATT after January 1995 to include a paragraph committing to "acceptable labour standard".

Developing countries, on the other hand, at the leadership of India were vehemently opposing US move by arguing that multilateral trading environment would be highly vitiated if any attempt was made to link between the trade and non-trade issues like human rights, labour standard and environment. Developing countries wanted the labour issue to be discussed in the International Labour Organisation (ILO) which was the specialised agency for this purpose. The West opined ILO was an ineffective talking shop for discussing any kind of serious issues. Therefore, it would be best if these issues were to be addressed through WTO. US call for labour standard had been followed by threat against China over its human rights record and against Indonesia for allegedly failing to protect workers' rights. India will obviously be the next target.

On labour standard, the US argument is that labours are highly underpaid in the developing countries. Due to lower real wage their products are much price competitive comparable to their developed counterparts which enable them to export and thus capture markets of the developed countries because the latter's markets are characterised by high price due to higher real wage. Though USA and France had reached a consensus in the G-7 meeting to put this issue at the top of the agenda, UK has not supported this idea. Moreover, Mr. Peter Sutherland, the Director General, has expressed strong reservations about US move in linking trade with the newly raised non-trade issues, what the West calls "Social Dumping". He opined that linking between these two issues would jeopardise the entire progress of the Uruguay Round of negotiations that had been achieved so far since its inception in 1986.

The issue of "Social Clause" had been extensively discussed in the G-15 meeting in New Delhi recently. All the participating countries expressed grave concern about the US motivation to fix minimum labour standards. They have argued that the main reason behind recent spurt in Foreign Direct Investment (FDI) to developing countries is to exploit cheap labour resource from the LDCs. If USA tries to standardise wages between developed and developing countries then not only this trend (FDI) will be arrested, but also thwarts the export drive of developing countries which is based on cheap labour resource. Second line of argument is that wage rate of any country is determined by its own economic strength and market affordability which is unrelated to wage rate of other countries. The determinants of wages are different in different countries. Finally, USA was not successful in getting it included in the agenda of WTO, but became successful in putting it as an agenda in the Preparatory Committee of the WTO. This issue can only be taken as an agenda to the WTO, subject to the approval of all contracting parties unanimously but this is hardly believable becuase developing countries have been resisting this idea right from the beginning.

Another important outcome of the Marrakesh treaty which has favourable implication for India is the removal of all quota restrictions on handloom exports to the United States. In return for this gesture, USA wants India to open its textile markets to foreign companies for high value added textile products. They argue that the average tariff rate on textile products in the US market is 10 per cent, whereas India's textile market is protected by as high as 50 per cent average tariffs. They want the reduction and binding of Indian tariff rates at levels not higher than 35 per cent for apparel, 30 per cent for fabrics and made-ups, 15 per cent for yarns and 7.5 per cent for fibre. Furthermore, they want India to eliminate all non-tariff barriers within three years and a commitment that no new tariff barriers will be established.

GATT PROPOSAL: IMPLICATIONS FOR INDIA'S RICE EXPORTS

DR. (MRS.) VIJAYA KATTI
Associate Professor,
Indian Institute of Foreign Trade

The GATT Agreement calls for reduction in export subsidies, internal support and market access barriers. Where imports had been banned a country must allow imports at a minimum rate of 3% initially of domestic consumption of the banned product climbing to 5% by the end of six years. All quotas and other hidden barriers must be converted to tariffs and progressively reduced. The existing tariffs and new tariffs resulting from tariffication must be reduced by 36% on an average over the six year phase-in-period in industrial countries with a minimum reduction of 15% for each tariff line item. In the area of internal support, trade distorting farm subsidies must be cut by 20% from 1986-88 base period levels allowing credit for farm support reduction undertaken since 1986.

This paper aims at examining the increased competitiveness of India's rice because of these three critical issues in GATT proposal. An attempt is made to explore the potential for India's rice exports especially because reduction in subsidies would raise the price of rice in countries like EC and Japan, making India's rice more competitive. The possibility of increasing the rice exports because of opening up of the Japanese market is also assessed. The issues related with rice exports with reference to US, EC and Japanese markets are also highlighted and strategic response of India in the light of GATT proposal which would increase the export potential of Indian rice because of low cost of production as well as opening up of new markets for rice will also be suggested.

Indian Rice Exports

India possesses a unique advantage in rice exports because of basmati rice which has a strong market developed due to good quality and the taste for it. Long grain, soft texture, non-stickiness with good cooking quality and the aromatic character has been the hallmark of Indian basmati rice. The bulk of the exports are to the Middle-East. A small percentage is exported to the European Countries and North America.

International Rice market is undergoing rapid changes and prospects for Indian rice exports are bright. Though India is the second largest producer, she ranks ninth in the list of rice exporters in the world. (Table 1). Table 2 reveals that India's rice exports have increased from Rs. 350 crores in 1988-1989 to Rs. 428 crores in 1989-90 and further to Rs. 900 crores in 1992-93. The figures for April-December 1993-94 show that Indian exports touched the figure of Rs. 800 crores in 6 months time so that one can safely assume they would touch Rs. 1200 crores or more in the current fiscal year. India's exports of non-Basmati rice have not grown very substantially in past because of attractive domestic price.

Pakistan has been the only rival/competitor of India in basmati rice exports. Pakistan has twice the area under basmati and its basmati production is close to three times that of India. Pakistan exports 25% of its basmati rice production. It is much more than the total exports of basmati by India. Most of the basmati rice in Pakistan has longer grain than Indian basmati but does not compare well with the Indian variety like 370 in aroma and cooking. Because of this reason, the Indian basmati 370 fetches higher price than Pakistani basmati. Countries like Saudi Arabia and UAE have switched to Pak basmati because of large price difference between the two varieties but the buyers of USA and UK increasingly favour and prefer Indian basmati due to its superior quality (Table 3).

The government has identified rice as one of the extreme focus areas for exports and has taken a few decisions because of which India should be able to play a significant role among the leading rice exporters of the world in the next three or four years. By a public notice on January 3, 1994, the government has dropped the MEP (Minimum Export Price) condition for export of basmati rice and reduced the MEP for superfine non-basmati rice from $ 225 to $ 200 per tonne. The decision is in tune with the competition in international markets especially in the lucrative gulf market. Pakistan is believed to be the only competitor of India for basmati rice. Its export price is around $ 450 per tonne. An MEP of $ 550 for Indian rice was hampering exports. Other steps include abolition of quota system in basmati allowing free movement of grains within the country and removal of stock limit.

For non-basmati exports, India needs to explore the markets in the African continent. India is conspicuous in these markets by its absence and with lowered MEP for non-basmati, the scope for entering and concentrating efforts towards making our rice acceptable to the African consumer taste-wise and price-wise are bright and efforts need to be made for encouraging the Indian exporters to undertake steps in this direction.

GATT Accord; Implications for India's Rice Exports

The GATT Agreement envisages gradual reduction of barriers of protectionist measures across the world by reducing farm subsidies and export subsidies trimming the tariffs and provision of minimum cost price to signatory nations. This Agreement is bound to bring about the quantitative and qualitative changes in world trade giving a boost to rice trade. This will certainly increase the scope for India's rice exports.

According to Anderson and Tyres[1] if food policies of OECD countries were completely liberalised international food prices would rise 30 per cent. Food self-sufficiency in 1995 would be 92 instead of 105 per cent in OECD countries and self-sufficiency in developing countries would be 104 instead of 95 per cent.

World agriculture is subsidised to the tune of 18 per cent of its value, with a range extending from 72.5 per cent in case of Japan, 26 per cent in case of EC and 36 per cent of value in case of US. With GATT proposal, world agriculture is expected to move to the developing countries. Indian agriculture is likely to prosper, inviting more resources purely on efficiency grounds.

Impact of reduction in subsidies

A reduction in subsidies would lead to increase in prices but, over time, the price responsiveness of supply and demand would moderate the increase in prices. The withdrawal of subsidies in Japan would raise the world prices of rice. However according to a recent study by Pursell and Gulati world prices of rice are expected to be depressed by Indian exports. Export markets demand high quality rice with broken percentages which substitute imperfectly for the predominant poorer quality rice (mainly about 20% broken) sold in domestic markets. The optimum export tax and optimum level of exports will depend on this price depressing effect (*i.e.* the elasticity of excess demand), the extent of the exchange rate overvaluation and the level of the non-traded subsidies (irrigation, electricity and credit) to rice growing. The study further expects subtantial export earnings ($ 1 billion for 3 mn. tonnes) in a short time with a moderate increase in domestic prices (say 10% to 20%).

The effects on world prices of implementing the Dunkel proposals have been comprehensively modelled by Brandao and Martin (1993) and they have arrived at the conclusion that reduction of positive protection tends to increase world prices and reducing negative protection increases supply and reduces world prices. For example, the reduction of rice protection in countries such as Japan, Korea and Indonesia would increase world prices but reducing the substantial discrimination against rice production in China and India would reduce world prices. In most of the Brandao and Martin Simulations as well as in earlier models, this effect predominates as regards rice.[2]

1. *Agricultural Trade Liberalisation, Implications for Developing Countries*, Ed. Ian Goldin and Odin Kndsen, OECD, Paris, 1990, p. 52.
2. Garry Pursell, Gulati, A., "Liberalising Indian Agriculture – An Agenda for Reform", *Working Papers Trade Policy*, World Bank.

Increased Competitiveness of India's Rice

As far as competitiveness of Indian rice is concerned, Indian rice is competitive and the extent of competitiveness would increase because of the withdrawal of state support. According to Mr. Gulati's study[3] the US has PSE (Producers Subsidy Equivalent) of 26.17 per cent, EC of 37 and Japan has PSE equivalent to 72.5 in case of rice. Thus to the extent of withdrawal of subsidy, there is a possibility of rise in price of rice of India which is taxing the farmers in production of rice. So the farmers would gain. However, India's competitors, Thailand and Pakistan, are also taxing their rice producers. So they would also gain and how far India will be able to compete with them needs to be seen. According to IIFT study on Wheat and Rice Exports rice is expected to be highly competitive compared to wheat. NPC for non-basmati rice for 1992-93 was estimated to be 47 and the study concludes that opening of external trade in rice will augment the income of the farmers.[4] IIFT Study has calculated the benchmark FOB export price of non-basmati rice (average 25% broken) for March 1992 at $198. It further states that this can be compared with the Thai White Rice 25% broken FOB Bangkok price which was $242 in March 1992. On the basis average price also, it is found that rice is expected to be highly competitive.

Japanese Market

Because of the opening of the Japanese market in immediate future, Indian rice will not be able to get a foothold mainly because of the taste of Japanese for Japonica variety which is short grain and sticky. It is not that India has not been growing this variety. But India does not possess comparative advantage in this particular rice. Moreover, the competitive edge for basmati exports is quite paying. The price for this particular rice is high, demand elasticity is very low and the stickiness of the market for this variety exists. However, there is every possibility that exports of Vietnam and Thailand to Japan would increase and because of that these two countries would vacate some of the markets in which India stands a very strong chance of entering. The strategic options open in this context need to be examined carefully and the action plan needs to be chalked out, taking into consideration the moves which would be undertaken by our competitors like USA, Vietnam and Thailand in this connection.

Japan had protected its markets for more than 4 decades and for the first time it has been forced by domestic compulsion as well as international

3. Gulati, A., Sharma, A.N., "Subsidising Agriculture, A Cross Country View", *Economic and Political Weekly*, September 26, 1993, p. 109.
4. B. Bhattacharya et al, *Study on Feasibility of Rice & Wheat Exports*, Indian Institute of Foreign Trade, April, 1992.

pressures to allow substantial imports this year. It expects to import a total of 2 million tonnes of rice before the end of the year thus becoming the world's largest rice importing country in this year. Japan has also agreed to open up this market in order to provide minimum cost price to agricultural products from other countries as per the GATT Agreement. Under this Agreement, Japan will import 4% of its domestic consumption gradually rising to 8%. This makes Japanese imports worth 4 lakh tonnes in 1995 which will gradually rise to 8 lakh tonnes in 1999. Obviously this will lead to a big jump in global rice exports.

Due to GATT agreement, a potential 500,000 tonnes market is foreseen by US exporters to Japan. The nearly 10 mn. tonnes Japanese market is a mdedium grain market but Japanese market could and would undergo a change in favour of long grain rice after the imports are liberalised. US, EC and Australia – the major exporters of medium grain rice – will be able to sell to opened Japanese markets only through cut backs in sale in other markets as prospects for further production expansion of rice are limited with Australia and EC as their production is already at record levels. Water constraints are likely to impede significantly further expansion of rice production in Australia and USA in near future. Farmers of South Korea and Thailand are expected to produce at a lower price and capture Japanese market with Japonica rice.

Thai rice is selling at US $400 per MT at present. India has reduced MEP for both basmati as well as non-basmati to $ 200. Moreover, Thailand may have smaller surplus for export next year because of current water scarcity there. This might give an opportunity to India to have a breathing time and a foothold in the unaccustomed markets.

The EC Market

The EC employs a variable levy (import duty) and subsidy system to protect and assist its own production. To protect EC production (mainly Italy, Spain, France, Greece), the levy is charged on all imported rice. It is the difference between the threshold price and the lowest world bid on that day. Levies are different for different varieties of rice. Important for Indian exports is the duty differential between white and brown rice. Long grained white rice from India attracts a duty of approximately $ 500 per tonne whereas the brown rice has a levy of about $ 300 per tonne. Due to large duty differential brown rice is largely exported to Europe.

EC production is 2.162 m. tonnes with imports of 1.1 m. tonnes and exports of 0.4 m tonnes. Under conditions of trade liberalisation perhaps half of that production would cease to be efficient; in particular, the French rice industry might survive but the Spanish and Italian rice industries would be under serious threat. An additional 1 m. tonne of long grain rice would be imported to the EC as demand increases in response to the sustained lower prices[5]. US production in particular would benefit because European consumer preference would stay with it, but there is every possibility of dramatic expansion of imports of close substitutes from Thailand (100 B Surinam). The EC produces about 2 m. tonnes of rice annually, mainly medium and short grain, whereas it consumes mainly imported long grain rice.

EC regulation allows the import of brown rice without import tax and the export of an equivalent amount of milled rice without subsidy. The export can also take place before the import. The EC has also introduced in 1991 a three year production subsidy to farmers who switch to growing long grain rice (indica) instead of less appreciated round grain varieties (Japonica).

EC single market prices for rice are well above the prices charged by the major producers for similar qualities – most notably the USA and Thailand. After liberalisation, the prices would increase further due to which trade may switch from EC market to non-EC markets. Depending upon US increasing exports to Japan, EC market would get vacated and India can enter EC market.

In the EC market, UK is the largest importer of Indian rice – mainly basmati. France and Germany import a lot of Indian non-basmati long-grained rice. There is large duty differential between white and brown rice – on an average duty for white rice is $ 580 per tonne and for brown rice is $ 350 per tonne. To circumvent the tariff wall, it is recommended to process/mill the rice within Europe.

EC's grain market is highly protected. There is intervention price which allow EC institutions to buy paddy from the farmers. The husking allowance (normally 25% of the cost of the paddy) is added to this alongwith a marketing component which includes advertising, milled rice, packing and transportation cost.[6] The total of these is called threshold price. This threshold price is normally much higher than the c.i.f. price for the rice of comparable variety. EC long grain varieties grown mainly in Italy (Arborio, Riberingo and Roma) do not conform to international definition of long grain rice (their length-width ratio is 2:1 whereas international ratio is 3:1). Moreover, they are sticky and chewy when cooked. EC charges include the premium with the imported rice and get over the local grain varieties. This amount is trimmed as external correcting amount. The difference between the threshold price and c.i.f. price of the imported price + external correction amount gives the import levy.

---

5. Roche, Julian, The International Rice Trade, Woodhead Publishing Ltd., Cambridge, England, 1992.

6. Mathur, Priya, *Report on Export Potential of High Value Rice with special reference to the European Market*, IIFT, 1993.

Such a calculation of import levy ensures that the price at which the imported long rice is available in the EC markets is so high that it is even more than the premium that a consumer is ready to pay for imported rice variety. The import levy on long grain rice is as high as 100 % to 350% because of which EC consumers prefer the EC grain to rice imported with tariffs. The EC imports around 7.5 lakh tonnes of rice from non-EC countries of which 3.8 lakh tonnes are accounted for by long grain imports. India can definitely tap this market if the import levies are reduced. Levy concessions granted to India have been very low. Moreover even the 25% concessions granted to Indian and Pakistani exporters is usually cornered by the importing traders and intermediate bodies. Basmati imports in the EC are to the tune of 70, 000 tonnes and if the levy is brought down to a more realistic levels, it would reach an export of 1.2 lakh tonnes. Indian rice. *i.e.* basmati enjoys a quota premium though not a cost advantage. India would be competitive in foodgrains but the policy makers need to remember that compared to other lower cost economies like Australia or Canada, it may not become that competitive. Hence the strategic response is absolutely essential keeping in view some of the problems being faced by the rice exporters which are noted below:

1. Purchase tax on paddy in Haryana and Punjab is being opposed by the farmers, abolition of which is calculated to bring down our prices by $ 60 per tonne thereby enhancing our competitiveness in the world markets.

2. Kandla happens to be one of the most important ports of India with ideal geographical location. Congestion at Kandla Port adds to increase in the freight rates by about 4 to 80 dollars per tonne.

3. Levy of 75% imposed on non-basmati is argued to be making our non-basmati non-competitive in the international market.

4. EC Rice and Agricultural Policy: India's basmati needs to be treated as special aromatic variety especially because of its quality and it could not be treated at par with any long grain variety.[7]

The US Market

Although USA is a principal exporter of rice, it is also importing more rice. The reason for this is increasing product differentiation within the US market. US Asians are not necessarily prepared to eat US rice on a regular basis. So US imports have increased eight times, from 20700 tonnes in 1980-81 to 160,000 tonnes in 1990-91 – currently approximately 6% of domestic production.[8] The increase in US rice imports reflects the growth in demand for more carbohydrates in the US diet, an increased demand for foreign,

7. *Economic Times*, 24-1-94.

8. *The International Rice Trade*, Julian Roche, Noodherd Publishing Ltd, Cambridge, England, 1992.

especially Asian foods and meals and a more sophisticated consumer awareness of alternative rice types. These factors have given rise to a growing market niche which US production has generally not supplied.

US response to the growing demand for speciality rices is obvious because of the introduction of the Jasmine 85 variety into Southern states and high quality Japanese style Japonica, M 401 into California recently. These market niches are comparatively small but their growth should provide the basis for further investigation into the potential for US production of speciality rices that can be competitively produced, milled and processed in the USA. Until this occurs, growth in rice imports can be expected to follow the trend in the 1980s, which implies that 10% of domestic consumption will be met from imports by 1995.[9]

Conclusions : India's rice is competitive in the world market and with the GATT Agreement, its competitiveness is expected to increase. With the opening of Japanese market, India's rice exports stand a chance to gain foothold in markets which US would be vacating due to increased exports to Japan. The taste of the Japanese for India's rice may get developed in the long run for which concentrated efforts will have to be made. Also increased prices due to reduction of subsidies in EC, US, Japan, will enhance India's competitiveness in terms of prices and India stands a chance to increase exports in these markets. The markets of South Africa and Middle East need to be conquered by systematic efforts. The problems faced by rice exporters need to be looked into. India stands a fair chance of becoming a major player in the rice market in the near future.

9. Roche, *op. cit.*

TABLE 1

World Rice Exports

(1989-93)

Quantity : 000 M/Tons

COUNTRY	1989	1990	1991	1992	1993
THAILAND	6036	3937	3993	4000	4400
USA	2967	2420	2197	2150	2300
VIETNAM	1400	1500	1000	2000	1700
EC-12	963	990	1090	1085	920
PAKISTAN	779	904	1297	1200	900
CHINA	320	300	689	750	700
INDONESIA	104	50	0	100	500
AUSTRALIA	450	470	400	550	500
INDIA	450	500	600	500	450
URUGUAY	251	250	262	300	350
TAIWAN	68	50	200	200	200
BURMA	456	86	300	200	200
ARGENTINA	130	70	125	250	175
EGYPT	100	32	85	160	170
GUYANA	26	30	53	55	75
S. KOREA	175	75	0	0	0
OTHERS	419	362	108	402	647
TOTAL	15094	12126	12699	14502	14187

TABLE 2

Export of Rice From India

YEAR	*Basmati*		*Non-basmati*	
	Qty.	Value	Qty.	Value
1987-88	3, 66, 081	339.95	22, 808	12.37
1988-89	3, 49, 687	333.53	35,753	20.23
1989-90	3, 96, 895	412.09	26, 705	16.36
1990-91	2, 41, 674	287.31	2, 93, 314	169.39
1991-92	2, 28, 588	429.92	5, 25, 790	320.07
1992-93	2, 86, 170	699.83	2, 76, 735	198.15
1993-94 (APR-DEC)	3, 28, 169	742.55	1, 12, 904	116.97
1993-94 (estimate)	4,00,000	960.00	1,60,000	140.00

Source: DGCI&S, Calcutta.

TABLE 3
GROWING BASMATI EXPORTS FROM INDIA

Year	Qty. (MT)	Value Rs. Crores	Unit Value Rs./MT
	SAUDI ARABIA		
1990-91	154,080	179.07	11622
1991-92	166,794	305.42	18311
1992-93	207,636	482.95	23028
	U.A.E.		
1990-91	16,884	22.17	13131
1991-92	16,935	31.96	18872
1992-93	19,203	50.27	26178
	KUWAIT		
1990-91	9,739	11.35	11654
1991-92	5,401	13.80	25551
1992-93	14,819	47.30	31919
	U.S.A.		
1990-91	4,325	7.23	16717
1991-92	3,462	8.50	24552
1992-93	3,909	14.47	37017
	CANADA		
1990-91	1,013	1.62	15992
1991-92	888	2.30	25901
1992-93	1,292	4.44	34365
	EUROPE		
1990-91	24,959	29.47	11807
1991-92	27,792	53.31	19182
1992-93	27,976	74.77	26726

STRATEGIC RESPONSE TO URUGUAY ROUND : A CONCEPTUAL APPROACH

B. BHATTACHARYYA,

Professor,

Indian Institute of Foreign Trade

Any analysis of strategic response in the post-Uruguay Round (UR) period must necessarily start with the question – response by whom, because strategy is formulated by each player after a scrutiny of the options available. Therefore, by definition there cannot be any generic strategic response. Who are the major players in this scenario? Essentially there are five and each one has distinct constituent, role and options, though there are intensive interface among them, as the Fig. 1 shows. Transaction-makers has been used to include the entire spectrum of economic activity, *viz*., industry and agriculture, both tradables & non-tradables, and trading.

The straight line relationships are possibly self-explanatory. The dotted lines show the possible strategic alliances which might develop even among players with divergent interests on specific occasions. For example, national and foreign Governments can come together to reduce the supervisory powers of GATT or multilateral application of international trade rules. Similarly, transaction-makers, independent of their locations, can form alliances with a view to extract premium from consumers.

Response is a derivative of perceived benefits or losses. If Government is the surrogate for the country, there is no doubt that Government will as a whole gain from the UR. But the general observation made in newspapers on

Fig. 1

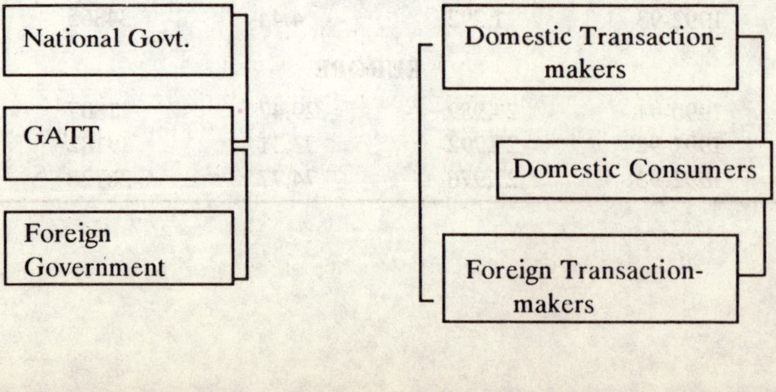

the quantitative magnitude of the gains appears to be incorrect. The figure is estimated by applying India's share to the expansion in world trade due to UR. This is not justified first because if UR is to be a success, it must represent a discontinuity and second, national shares in world trade should change as national efforts to actualise the potential gains cannot be expected to be uniform, apart from the non-linear distribution of the tradable product matrix across nations.

Transaction-makers as a generic group also will gain – in fact, what is gain for the country is gain for them. The only difference is that these will be sub-sectoral losses and gains. And response will vary accordingly.

The only group which is expected to lose out is that of domestic consumers at least in the short run. This will be because of at least two factors. First, there will be increase in prices of pharmaceuticals. Though the extent of increase can be debated, there is no point in denying that there would be increase; had there be no escalation, the patent-holders would be least interested in this long drawn fight any way. Second, there will be increase in prices of agricultural products. Indian agriculture has so far been given negative protection. Now that agriculture will be opened up, – supplemented by export delicensing – prices of agricultural output in India will gravitate towards international level. Result will be increase in the income of the agricultural producers which will partially come from higher domestic prices to be paid by domestic consumers.

Given this balance sheet of perceived gains and losses, what could be the strategic responses to the Uruguay Round of each player? That would require a much larger scope of analysis than what this paper will permit which intends to consider only one of the players, *viz.*, domestic transaction-makers of producers type. But since they will have to accept as a datum the new policy regime as determined by the domestic Government's strategic responses, let us briefly consider what these could be.

It may be best to start with what is not a strategic response. Whatever the Government of India will do as a legal obligation under the Uruguay Round is not a strategic response, *e.g.*, reduction in tariff or changes in the Patent Law. In contrast, whatever policy adjustments it initiates either for greater utilisation of the UR-triggered global market access conditions or damage limitation caused by the package which was imposed, are strategic responses.

What could be the strategic responses of the domestic transaction-makers to the Uruguay Round? Before any answer to this question is attempted, it should be appreciated that this Round has been concluded at a time when the Indian economy has already been exposed to certain liberalisation measures which, in fact, were mostly centred on Trade and Foreign Direct Investment.

The Uruguay Round in this context becomes only another dimension of the overall process of the integration of India with the global economy.

The real issue is, therefore, how do the transaction-makers decide on their strategic responses with a paradigm shift, from a quasi-command economy to a market-driven economy, because what the UR tries to achieve is to liberalise cross-border transactions in goods and services within a transparent, rule-based, multilaterally administered system.

International Business literature provides a framework for analysing the strategic response of the industry based on the concept of shelter. Since an inward locking, restrictive policy regime provides shelter to the domestic industry from external competition, it is axiomatic that the industrial sub-sectors enjoying a high degree of shelter will resist the liberalisation process, whether it is due to Government policies or commitment to GATT under UR. Conversely, there will also be sub-sectors which are relatively more export-oriented. An import-substitutive policy is discriminatory to export-industries, as it introduces distortions reducing efficiency. These sub-sectors will welcome the liberalisation process in the domestic policy regime as well as the global marketing opportunities due to UR (Fig. 2).

		Shelter Enjoyed: High	Shelter Enjoyed: Low
Export Orientation	High	?	Most enthusiastic to Reforms/GATT
	Low	Least enthusiastic	Complacent

Fig. 2

The focus for action will have to be where the interests of the Government and the industry converge and, therefore, collective and consensual policy and programmes could be developed and implemented. These areas are:

(i) the industrial sub-sectors which have already emerged as globally competitive or are poised for such a role, *e.g.*, textiles, garments, engineering;

(ii) the industrial sub-sectors which will get adversely affected by the UR results and the Government would like to take corrective action in the context of social welfare, *e.g.*, pharamaceuticals;

(iii) the sectors/products which will enjoy enhanced market access opportunities due to the Round but exploitation of which will require a more enabling environment, *viz.*, agriculture, off-shore development of softwear.

Before any package of actions could be conceptualised, the 'objective' which these actions would achieve has to be specified. While multiple objectives can obviously be formulated, it is good to remember that greater is the multiplicity, higher is the probability of inner inconsistency among the set of objectives. It will be, therefore, pragmatic to reduce the number of objectives. The two objectives – one each for Government and transaction-makers – can be formulated as priority:

1. To maximise the gains from UR-triggered global market access possibilities, while minimising the adverse impact on domestic production/prices (for the Government).
2. To emerge as international players in their respective areas of operation (for the transaction-makers). For the industry, it can specifically be stated as 'emergence as multinational enterprise'.

It is evident that these objectives are internally consistent and, therefore, there will be 'partnership' attitude between the industry and Government towards any set of strategic actions targeted to the attainment of the twin objectives.

It should also be emphasized that in the context of the current policy reforms, the role of the Government as a direct transaction-maker is on the wane. Therefore, the new role model will be that of a facilitator, essentially in creating an enabling environment. And, therefore, the first part of the governmental objective, *viz.*, maximising the gains from the UR will have to be achieved through the trade and industry, while the Government creates the environment. This is equally true of the second part of the governmental objective.

Given this objective, what should be the policy/promotional framework for the Government?

(i) Eliminate/minimise any anti-export bias still remaining in the macro policy regime.

(ii) Develop an appropriate import policy which is neutral. Since the economic objective is to make Indian industry and agriculture globally competitive as a whole, the concept of import policy for registered exporters becomes invalid.

(iii) Avoidance of an import policy regime which provides incentives to exporters through schemes such as Special Import Licenses, will make the import process, including the customs angle, less rigorous, as need for control and monitoring would be less. A transparent and efficient importation process is more critical for globalisation process, including offshore trading, than the marginal incentives that could be passed on through the import policy in the long run.

(iv) Step up investment in sectors where externalities predominate, and whose efficiency will influence substantially corporate ability to perform in external sector. These are essentially power, transport and telecommunication.

(v) Above all, change the mind set. Follow what the Economist describes as the new policy that is being thought of for the Ministry of International Trade & Industry of Japan: "(It) talks of revising the Japanese view that anything not explicitly permitted by law requires bureaucrats permission. In future, firms should forge ahead so long as what they do is not explicitly prohibited."

What should be the strategic response of the industry?

(vi) Appreciate two important new postulates: first, the domestic market can no longer be considered as protected and, therefore, only way to survive is to strive for a level of efficiency which will bring it to the world level. Second, the Government's ability to come as a saviour on a permanent basis even for export purpose will be strictly limited due to both the commitment to GATT and the market determined approach being followed by the Government.

This is not too difficult a task for industries which have so far been receiving less shelter but would require substantial effort on the part of the heavily protected industries.

(vii) Develop proper R & D facilities which so far has been the weakest aspect of Indian industry. Even in pharmaceuticals, where the local industry may temporarily get adversely affected by the UR results, it can convert this setback in a winning situation by developing R & D in niches where foreign firms are not vitally interested, *e.g.*, tropical diseases. Focusing attention on such niches will be both nationally and internationally highly profitable.

What response is required where Government-industry collaboration is involved? Principally these are two:

(vii) Restructure the Export Promotion Councils and the Commodity Boards and set a new goal which is to convert these into industry-specific 'market promotion agencies'. So far these have been essentially incentive demanding and disbursing agencies. From now on, these should be instruments of market development in a corporate framework.

(ix) In association with industry, develop a framework and create a fund for launching potential global brands of Indian origin. The fund can be structured in such a way that it could be self-financing over a defined time-frame.

EMERGING OPPORTUNITIES IN THE SERVICES SECTOR

DR. K.V. SWAMINATHAN
Chairman (WITC)
and Adviser (APCTT), New Delhi.

Introduction

There is an accepted feeling that the developed countries have tremendous potential in the services sector and the developing countries are at the receiving end with very limited options to improve their position. The contribution of the services sector in the Gross Domestic Product (GDP) of the developed countries is relatively very high and often larger than the contribution of the industries to the GDP. Often the contribution of the services sector even in the least developed countries has been estimated to be over 1/3 of their GDP. In many developing countries which have a large agricultural sector the contribution to the GDP from the agriculture has been declining with increases coming from either industry sector and even more prominently from the services sector. In the Asia Pacific region very few countries have the services sector contributing less than 1/3 to the GDP; in the countries like Hong Kong and Singapore nearly 2/3 of the GDP comes from the services sector and in many of the Newly Industrialising Countries (NIC) the contribution of the services sector is almost 50%. In India, the distribution of the GDP between agricultural, industrial and the services sector is roughly spread as 25%, 35% and 40% respectively.

2. Developing countries suffer seriously in the inadequacies of the services and in dealing with them three issues may be kept in view. The first relates to problems in prioritisation. While this is likely to be country specific as well as industry specific, it appears that most of the developing countries have to bestow attention on adoption of infrastructure services such as transportation, telecommunication, utilities and banking; in the producer services attention to be shared among data services, R&D, engineering, consultancy, design, legal, advertising and insurance. There is also pressure on modernising the data processing and banking services. The second factor relates to the need for indigenous services production. Many services industry arc employment-oriented in the developing countries which usually have surplus potential and as such there is an emphasis in seeking services with interest on long term indigenisation; where inadequate capital resources and domestic market size are constraints importing such services from abroad are resorted to. The third factor relates to as to which form of import would be desirable to meet

the urgent needs of the services sector such as: foreign direct investment, non-equity forms of contract, BOT contracts, licensing and other franchising arrangements.

3. In a sense, the technology status is at the very core of services sector, the factor leading to international competitiveness. In view of the large R&D expenditure incurred by developed countries, particularly through the transnational corporations and the competitive environment they have exploited, their services sector is in a very dynamic stage incorporating the rapid technological advances. On the other hand, many developing countries are not able to allocate adequate responses to meet the technological needs of the services sector and as such widening service gaps are emerging between developed and developing countries.

4. International trade in different form contains components relating to the services sector. Four elements can easily be recognised in this context : (i) In tradable goods there is an element of service content. Due to the technological changes taking place the producer services are crucial in the production processes and the material content of the goods. In fact the service content of goods is likely to play a determining role in the competitive advantage of the tradable goods produced. (ii) In package deals goods and services are combined and this is more so in hightech and high value added products. The competitive advantage in such packages is often determined by the service components. (iii) Support activities required to sustain a market, particularly to ensure the products sold perform the functions for which they have been purchased require a well orchestrated and an efficient services sector. (iv) In many cases some of the services are tradable by themselves. Wide range of services involving qualified and skilled personnel such as Consultancy, Accounting, Legal and other Business services rendered by professionals are examples of services that can be traded directly.

5. The recently concluded Uruguay Round of multilateral trade negotiations include [in Annexure (l.b)] the agreement reached on trade in services.

6. Banking, Insurance, Shipping and Communications are by now well known service sectors. Most of these sectors, in India were in the public sector and as such its reluctance to open up these sectors to foreign enterprises. However, with the recent liberalisation moves the position has changed considerably. Narasimhan Committee Report on Banking and Malhotra Committee Report on Insurance and Chellaiah Committee Report on Taxation have indicated the direction of future movements. Many other service sectors are also potentially attractive which includes in particular Construction and Design Engineering services, Business and Professional services in many critical areas. This paper examines opportunities that will emerge in the

immediate future, particularly for services involving Engineering Design and related technical skills.

Indian Consultancy Scene

7. The number of consultancy organisations and consultants is well over 3000 and with a turnover of Rs. 1000 crores annually. They have also contributed in addition to about Rs. 130 crores on consultancy exports. It employs over 100,000 Specialists including about 10,000 in management consultancy. The spectrum of discipline and services provided by the consultancy in India cover a very wide range. They have also rendered services starting with project identification to supervision of construction and commissioning supplemented with a wide range of services on personnel, material and financial management, market survey, rehabilitation of sick units, as well as operation and maintenance. The consultancy organisations in India are directly or indirectly supported by more than 500 R&D Institutions and Research Laboratories in the country including the chain of national laboratories both under the CSIR as well as other major scientific organisations such as DRDO, Atomic Energy and Space. Some consultancy organisations have also closely worked with the Indian Institute of Technology, Universities and faculty of management institutions. Financial Institutions like IDBI, IFCI and ICICI have also promoted consultancy by establishing State level consultancy organisations to provide services to entrepreneurs in their respective areas.

8. The types of consultancy organisations in the country could be grouped on the basis of the ownership and these would include: (*i*) public sector consultancy organisation like Engineers India Limited (EIL) in the area of Petro-Chemicals, Metallurgical and Engineering Consultancy Organisation (MECON) and Rail India Technical and Economic Services (RITES); (*ii*) captive consultancy organisations have been established by large private sector industrial houses and examples of such include Tata Consultancy Services (TCS), Tata Energy Research Institute (TERI) and Kirloskar Consultants; (*iii*) there are over 1000 small and medium independent consultancy organisations in the private sector with specialisation in specific areas; (*iv*) there are 18 technical consultancy organisations backed by major financial institutions providing techno-economic and techno-managerial consultancy services; (*v*) institutional consultancy organisations include those which are attached to well known institutions in the country like Foundation for Innovation and Technology Transfer (FITT) of the IIT, National Productivity Council (NPC), National Industrial Development Corporation (NIDC) etc; (*vi*) a large number of retired professionals who have acquired knowledge are working as freelance consultants and perhaps their number could be around 50,000; (*vii*) In-house consultants – large organisations like Power Corporation,

Electricity Boards, Road Transport Corporations draw on the expertise acquired by their senior staff even after their retirement; and (*vii*) NRIs settled in developed countries who have access to the latest technology are showing interest in providing inputs on commercial basis to organisations in India and in this manner they could enhance the level of performance of Indian counterparts making them competitive.

9. The consultancy organisations in India are well placed to serve as technology carriers in a wide range of activity including those involving import of technology, technology upgradation within the country as well as export of technology. In view of the very large and varied domestic markets the Indian consultancy has acquired a unique feature in its capability for technology evaluation, transfer and absorption to suit local conditions. They are also capable of scaling down and commercialising without serious compromises on quality and yield.

10. Export of consultancy services, one of the 14 thrust areas of export identified by the Government Activities during the 7th Plan period, resulted in actual growth of 25% in the export of consultancy services. During the 8th Plan period 30% growth is anticipated and Rs. 840 crores is the target in 1994-95 and Rs. 1000 crores in 1995-96. A major portion of the consultancy export is in the area of Software activity. While Indian consultancy had made its presence in export of services in more than 60 developing and developed countries, its share in international market is still very small – possibly about 1%. The consultancy organisations have already started laying emphasis on quality of services in recognition of the stiff competition in the international market.

11. Many Indian consultancy organisations and construction agencies have undertaken turnkey projects in many countries in Europe and Asia. Following the oil crisis in the 70s some of these agencies geared up effectively in winning several construction projects and they did receive appreciation from several quarters. However, the value of such contracts has declined considerably in the later half of 80s and several problems have been encounted in dealing with such project exports. This is a major area in which the consultancy will be closely linked with large developmental projects and as such returns from them could be substantial. It is expected that this area will receive close consideration from the government in taking full advantage of the Indian potential in meeting the large foreign market.

12. In January 1993 the Government of India issued its Technology Policy Statement (TPS) laying emphasis on strengthening design engineering capability. The Government of India examined the role of the consultancy in the country and created an institutional arrangement for supporting and encouraging technical consultancy by setting up the "Consultancy Development Centre"

(CDC) with the active cooperation of National association of Consulting Engineers (NACE), Association of Consulting Engineers (ACE) and Federation of Indian Export Organisations (FIEO). The CDC established in 1986 has taken a wide range of measures in strengthening the consultancy capability in the country. This nodal agency is now well geared to take more challenging tasks and would be playing a critical role in the emerging opportunities in the services sector.

Characteristics of Certain Services Sectors

13. The services sector covers a very wide range of services, each characterised by special features.

Engineering Design Services

14. Engineering Design Services determine the technology dimension of an investment project through the techno-economic specifications they produce for civil construction, the material to be used and machineries and equipments to be purchased. The engineering design services play an important role at the stage of pre-investment studies in translating an intention to an action plan. The second stage of engineering design services are performed after the pre-investment studies have been completed. At this stage, the services supply could include process and product design, architectural and structural design, design and layout, supervision of construction and equipment installation, testing of materials and equipment and quality control. The third stage would relate to project implementation services and could include production activities, training of technical and management personnel and maintenance.

Construction Services

15. The construction services are those for the physical construction of an investment project. They bring together labour, materials and equipments and translate the techno-economic specifications produced by the engineering design services into concrete physical units. The construction services make use of unskilled and semi-skilled labour in addition to specialised engineering and managerial personnel. It has been gathered that top 200 international design firms had a market of about 5 billion U.S. Dollars around 1990 with about 70% of the international market in developing countries. United States companies had a share of about 25% of this market and over 40% of the market being held by European companies. The 90% of the engineering design for this market was dominated by firms from the industrialised countries. Republic of Korea had a market of about 1.5%. The value of the construction services market assessed on the basis of the contracts awarded to some 250 top international contractors was of the order of about 100 billion dollars around 1990, considerably below the peek of 134 billion dollars in 1981. It

could be noticed that the value of the foreign construction contracts is about 20 times the Engineering Design services and as such substantial larger volumes of resources are influenced by a higher quality of engineering design. The domestic contracts of these 250 international contractors were about 3 to 4 times the value of foreign contracts. United States is still the world's largest exporter of service with their share at about 25%. It has also been noticed that in many cases large parts of the award of international construction contract have gone to contractors in those countries from where the engineering design services have been procured. This thus reinforces the need for the engineering design services in a country in order that it may succeed more and more in securing international contracts for development projects.

Telecommunication Services Sector

16. Due to several well known reasons the telecommunication services sector in almost all countries remain controlled both for the provision and for the use for domestic and international services. This sector has in fact a dual role: (i) as a distinct sector of economic activity; (ii) as the underlining transport media for other economic activities. Telecommunication is often referred to as Core services facilitating the delivery of services produced by other sectors as well as generating its own processing, transaction and delivery of services.

17. Telecommunications have been revolutionalised in the recent past by technological advances. Telecommunication is an electronic conduct used to transfer voice or data from point to point. This also has been used for mass diffusion in broadcasting. Digital technologies resulting from the convergence of communication and computing have created a new environment for services that are capable of being furnished from the same storage and transmission medium. Many users can share resources across network. The current situation where all types of data travel on highly defined and standardised part have been described as the world's digital highways. Technological progress has permeated the telecommunication segment very effectively. Computing processes for and storage capability have vastly increased; Digital switching capability are replacing mechanical equipments; Glass fibre transmission technology are replacing copper; widebands with higher transmission speeds are being introduced in many countries. As a result of such developments in telecommunication, it offers a very large bi-directional circuits for transcontinental communication. For example, INTELSAT has more than 100, 000 circuits and private transatlantic telecommunication cables has over 80,000 circuits. It thus appears that capacity would not be a constraint in international telecommunication facilities. The technological advances have also transformed historical barriers of location, time and

distance irrelevant. Location on land, sea or the air cutting across national boundaries are all now well connected. Telecommunication does not have character similar to many other services such as professional services, insurance and transportation. It has largely an indigenous sector servicing national needs but with world-wide linkages. The relationship between trade and development are extremely strong in the telecommunication sector.

Professional Business Services

18. Professional business services have a wide range of activities even though many of them have certain common characteristics. Professional business services are services that are primarily purchased by other producers for the purpose of being consumed in latest stages of production. The purchasers are generally firms and not individuals. Professional services are mostly in the business of delivering expertise calling for inputs from skilled professional, technical or managerial personnel. Professional business service comprises a mix of activities such as account, auditing, law, etc., which require some type of accredition and few others which are open to all like computer software, advertising and management consultancy.

19. Large firms have considerable advantage in providing a package of business services. However, many small firms specialised in specific sector are very competitive in view of the fact that they are able to access the delivery channels as comfortably as the large firms do. It has also been felt that the large business firms are potentially far more unstable than the manufacturing firms because of the technology location. Primarily in established manufacturing the technology is machine embodied whereas in business services they are people based.

20. Trade barriers of various types have been recognised in the process of internationalising business services. These include: restrictions on market access and on the right of parties; restrictions on the mobility of personnel; restrictions on technology transfer; restrictions on transporting data flows; restrictions on international payments; restrictions on national procurement; restrictions on the scope of business; restrictions on the use of the name of firms; and subsidies.

GATS

21. The Preamble of the General Agreement on Trade in Services (GATS) recognises the right of Members to regulate and introduce new regulations on the supply of services within their territories in order to meet national policy objectives and given asymmetries existing with respect to degree of development of services regulations in different countries, in particular the need of developing countries to exercise this right. This has also expressed the desires to

facilitate the increasing participation of developing countries in trade in services and the expansion of the services exports through the strengthening of their domestic capacity and its efficiency and competitiveness.

22. This has defined trade in services as the supply of services: from the territory of one country into the territory of any other country; in the territory of one country to the service consumer of any other country; by a service supplier of one country through commercial persence in the territory of any other country; and by a service supplier of one country through presence of natural persons of a country in the territory of any other country. This has excluded the services which are supplied neither on a commercial basis nor in competition with one or more suppliers.

23. Some of the salient features of GATS could be seen in Article II on Most Favoured Nation Treatment, Article IV on Increasing Participation of Developing Countries, Article V(*bis*) on Labour Markets Integration Agreements, Article VI on Domestic Regulations and Article VII on Recognition.

24. The Article on most favoured nation treatment has stated: with respect to any measure covered by this agreement each Member shall accord immediately and unconditionally to services and services suppliers of any other Member, treatment no less favourable than it accords to like services and service suppliers of any other country. It has also stated that this should not be so construed as to prevent any Member from conferring advantages to adjacent countries in order to facilitate exchanges limited to contiguous frontier Zones of services that are both locally produced and consumed. Article IV has stated that increasing participation of the developing countries in world trade shall be facilitated through negotiated specific commitments relating to: (a) the strengthening of the domestic services capacity and its efficiency and competitiveness *inter alia* through access to technology on a commercial basis; (b) The improvement of their access to distribution channels and information networks; and (c) the liberalisation of market access in sectors and modes of supply of export interest to them. It has also stated that developed country Members and to the extent possible other Members, shall establish contact points within two years from the entry into force of the agreement establishing the MTO to facilitate the access of developing countries' service suppliers to information related to their respective markets concerning: (a) commercial and technical aspects of the supply of services; (b) registration, recognition and obtaining professional qualifications; and (c) the availability of services technology.

25. On domestic regulations it has stated: with a view to ensuring that measures relating to qualification requirements and procedures about technical standards and licensing requirements do not constitute unnecessary barriers

to trade and services, the Council for Trade in Services shall through appropriate bodies it may establish, develop any necessary disciplines. The Article relating to Recognition states: a Member may recognise the education or experience obtained, requirements met or licences or certifications granted in a particular country. Such recognition which may be achieved through harmonisation or otherwise may be based upon an agreement or arrangement with the country concerned or may be accorded autonomously.

26. Part III on Specific Commitments has dealt with market access and national treatment. With respect to market access, each Member shall accord services and service suppliers of any other Member treatment no less favourable than that provided for under the terms, limitations and conditions agreed and specified in its schedule. On the National Treatment it states: in the sectors it has inscribed in its schedule and subject to any conditions and qualification set out therein each Member, shall accord to services and service suppliers of any other Member, in respect of all measures affecting the supply of services, treatment no less favourable than it accords to its own like services and service suppliers. Article XXV on technical cooperation has also explicitly stated that technical assistance to developing countries shall be provided at the multilateral level by the MTO Secretariat and shall be decided upon by the Council for Trade in Services.

27. The GATS has annexures on Article II exemptions, on movement of natural persons supplying services under the agreement, on financial services, on telecommunications and on air transport services and on negotiations on basic telecommunications.

Where India Stands?

28. In an overall assessment of the benefits that could accrue to India from GATS it is felt that there are several service sectors in which India will stand to gain. In particular, clear openings can be seen in the broad segment of construction and engineering design services, business and professional services as indicated in this paper earlier.

29. The enlarged opportunities for the services sector for Indian suppliers would arise mainly from three specific identifiable opportunities that have emerged : (i) Foreign investments have shown a remarkable increase in the recent past and this in turn would result in a much larger volume of projects to come in the near future. This will require engineering and design services to be followed by construction services at a very much larger level. Early action taken would result in a substantial part of engineering design services to be performed by Indian consultants which will eventually also lead to a large part of the construction services to be provided in the country. Since several new investors will be entering India for the first time this opportunity

should be taken full advantage of by Indian services system. It is also possible to visualise that once such contracts are established with new foreign investors Indian consultancy services would also more easily find acceptance in other countries where the same investors are likely to take part. The essential prerequisite for such favourable opportunities to be harvested would be the ability of the Indian services suppliers to be competitive, provide timely services and ensure a high quality performance. (ii) There is a tremendous export drive from India much of which could be related to new products that are to be exported. With every new product a considerable amount of design services from within the country are to be secured. This again should be taken advantage of, otherwise not only the opportunity of incorporating consultancy services in the product would be lost but eventually the export market itself may have to be surrendered to more competitive enterprises. (iii) The contribution for the services sector to the GDP in many countries of the world are increasing; with absolute increase in GDP itself, one could therefore expect very large increase in the demand for services all over the world and more so in many developing countries. India with its large scientific and technically qualified manpower should be able to mobilise a sizeable part of this for enlarging services. The essential prerequisite for this should be the ability of the Indian service suppliers to take full advantage of the technological advantages that have taken place and have been effectively incorporated in the services sector in a timely manner.

Concerns and Options

30. There are real concerns about the ability and speed with which Indian service suppliers would be able to establish commercial presence in other countries to deliver services. This is more so in view of the very high cost of office space, communication cost and staff salaries in foreign countries.

31. The following points may be examined to benefit from the services boom ahead :

(*i*) The developments in the telecommunication services will be critical in order that the Indian players in many service sectors will not be at a handicap compared to their competitors in other countries. It, therefore, appears that for substantial gains to accrue immediate attention should be given to improving the availability of telecommunication services in the country.

(*ii*) While subsidies are always likely to be frowned upon it is clear that considerable encouragement, in several identified segments of the domestic market where local enterprises are providing services, need to be provided as an interim measure to enable them to perform service functions in a competitive manner over a short period.

(*iii*) Indian service agencies particularly in the engineering design service sector need to establish early inter-linkages in other countries in order not to be handicapped through restrictions relating to market access or visa regulations. In United States and a part of Europe there are several NRIs who have established firms with whom Indian partners could cooperate in order to facilitate and speed up the process of establishing linkages.

(*iv*) As envisaged in the GATS one could expect contact points to be established in developed countries to access a vide range of services information. It appears that appropriate counterpart agencies in India should be established. Such contact points in India should ensure diffusion of such information through appropriate measures to a wide range of suppliers of services from India; this will enable not only an efficient diffusion system but as well will reduce the unit cost of such information to Indian customer. For example, the Consultancy Development Centre would act as a focal point in a wide range of information sourcing and distribution in the area of engineering design and construction.

(*v*) A wide range of training programmes are required to be prepared and an effective system evolved to have them conducted which will enable a large number of consultants and consultancy organisation in the country to participate and benefit therefrom. It should be possible that the consultancy agencies particularly the relatively smaller ones would then be able to join the main stream of competitive consultancy services.

To Sum up

32. The Indian consultancy exports had been targeted at about Rs. 1000 crores by 1995-96; however, in the light of the new emerging opportunities and the preparatory steps that India can take from now on could well change this figure to the order of Rs. 2000 to 3000 crores in 1995-96 and possibly target Rs. 10,000 crores per year by the turn of this century. To this should be added the services exports from several other segments identified; no doubt at all that such a figure will be very mcuh larger !

INTELLECTUAL PROPERTY PROTECTION – GETTING READY FOR THE FUTURE

DR. K.V. SWAMINATHAN
Chairman (WITC)
and Adviser (APCTT), New Delhi

Introduction

The creative work of the human mind is protected through several measures and the main motivation for the same is that such protection is a definite measure of encouragement for the creative activity. Several forms of protection of the creative activity have come about including those which are of particular interest in the industrial development. Scientific enquiry is at the very centre of a large part of the industry related creativity and is often strengthened by several other measures. These cover activities relating to manufacturing, use, sales and exports which are clearly seen to be in the domain of commerce and economics. Artistic and cultural attainments and innovations thereon, such as those embodied in art work and music are also being encouraged through such protection. While there are many categories of such protective measures that have come about, perhaps, Copyrights, Patents, Trademarks and Designs are known to have received recognition for a long time. Newer forms of protections are also emerging particularly stimulated by the more recent scientific and technological activities. Examples of such protection can be seen in the efforts made to protect computer programmes and softwares; life forms particularly following developments in Bio-Technology and protection of integrative circuits following developments in semi-conductors and micro electronics.

2. In the context of the recently concluded negotiations at GATT in Geneva containing the agreement on Trade Related aspects of intellectual Property Rights, a wide range of concerns and opportunities have been identified. This is so, because in the years ahead the global output will increase enormously and along with that the world trade would also increase substantially.

India is a party to the final act concluded at GATT. Whatever might have been India's role and contribution to the final act that has come about, what is now important is what advantage India can take from this for its own benefit and development.

3. This paper looks closely at one sub-set of the intellectual property

measures, namely Patents. This thus surveys the current Indian scene on patents, the role of Paris Convention and the Indian appreciation of the same and the salient feature of the GATT accord relating to patents. The paper then concentrates on some of the immediate steps for which India should prepare itself and work out some of the strategic measures it would take in getting ready for the future.

Indian Patent System

4. The origin of the Indian Patent System could be traced to the Act of 1856 granting exclusive privileges to inventors. At the time of independence in 1947 the Indian Patents and Designs Act of 1911 was in force. After prolonged considerations a new Patent Act came into being in 1970 and is now currently in force. From about 40,000 patents that were in force in 1968, this number has come down steadily and currently it is estimated that about 15,000 patents are in force. From over 5,000 patent applications filed annually in the late 60s, it is estimated that currently around 3,500 applications are being filed. The patent applications filed by Indians over this period has fluctuated from around 1000 to about 1300 annually and currently it is estimated that around 1100 patents are being filed. Indian Patent Act, 1970, while it had very little impact in the number of applications of Indians it did reduce the number of applications filed by the foreigners in India.

5. The Indian R&D expenditure over the last 25 years had increased by a substantial amount; in particular its allocations for the S&T sector during the successive Five Year Plans had also increased substantially. The in-house R&D activity in the country had also increased in a significant manner during the last decade. While the contributions made by the public and private sector scientific institutions are substantial from several considerations, their impact on the patent system has by and large been negligible. It is only in the very recent past serious efforts are being made, even now by very small number of agencies, for the scientific activities carried out in India to obtain patent protection in foreign countries.

6. The salient features in terms of the provisions contained in the Patent Act would broadly be seen in: areas which are not patentable; inventions where only methods or process of manufacture are patentable and not the products; conditions attached to the patent rights in particular provisions for important use by or for Government; provision for revocation and provisions for grant of compulsory licences; endorsement of "Licence of Right" in certain cases; and duration of patents.

Paris Convention

7. The World Intellectual Property Organisation (WIPO) administers

certain conventions relating to a wide range of subjects covered under the intellectual property matters, and in particular the Berne and Paris Convention. India is a member of the WIPO for about two decades. India is a member of the Berne Convention administered by WIPO and this convention deals with copyrights and related matters. India is not a member of the Paris Convention which deals with Industrial Property matters.

8. The Paris Convention was established in 1883 and it had undergone several revisions and the convention that is currently open is referred to as the Stockholm Revision (1967). There are over 100 member States who are parties to this convention. The Paris Convention which sets ground rules to ensure certain minimum standards of protection in the area of Industrial Property is available in countries who are members of the Convention. It should, however, be pointed out that it has no jurisdiction of its own in any country and in any given country only its own industrial property laws can be embraced.

9. The substantive provisions of the Paris Convention fall into three categories namely: national treatment, rights of priority and certain common rules. The national treatment is to ensure that the contracting States grant the same protection and same right to a patent of other States which it gives to its own nationals. Rights of priority in the Paris Convention provides that any inventor after making his first application in one of the contracting States may within a limited period file applications in other desired countries of the union and in such a case he will enjoy the benefit of the date of filing in all countries as done in the first country. In the case of patents this right of priority is 12 months and in the case of industrial property and trademark it is 6 months. This is a major benefit to the members of the Paris Union. Considering that the time required to comply with the procedure and regulation in different countries and possibly in different languages the inventor gets time to comply with the requirements. Further, during the rights of priority period the inventor may even carry out further investigations and experimentation and may confirm the utility of the invention for seeking patents in other countries.

10. There are a few common rules which the contracting State must follow and the more important among them are: (*i*) Independence of Patent; by this it is meant that the fact that the patent has been granted in a given country is not a ground for getting a patent in any other country. As such in each country its decision would be independent of those in any other country. (*ii*) The inventor has the right to be named in a patent. (*iii*) Even though there may be limitations in the domestic law in the use of certain products that will not be a ground for rejection of patents. (*iv*) The States may also take legislative measures for providing compulsory licences to prevent abuses as

for example, failure to work. However, a revocation cannot be given on the ground of failure to work except after issuing a compulsory licence.

11. It must however be mentioned that except for the provisions of the type indicated, the convention leaves free every contracting State to legislate as it wishes. For example, each State is free to exclude from patentability inventions belonging to certain fields of technology; to decide whether patent should be granted with or without examination as to the novelty and other criteria of patentability; to fix the duration of patents; the scope of a product patent, process patent or a combination of both; and all details of procedures and administration.

Background to the TRIPs in the Uruguay Round

12. There were attempts to revise the Paris Convention under the WIPO, starting with a resolution for the revision in 1974. However, much progress could not be made and as such the 1967 Stockholm text is still valid.

13. During the 1980s, however, international agencies and bodies showed considerable amount of interests on issues relating to Intellectual Property. Some developed countries had viewed industrial property right as critical for their economy and had felt that because of inadequate treatment they were loosing a large part of the R&D results which normally would have accrued to them. They had felt that a large part of the R&D activity which had given them a leadership position in technology was being eroded and many other countries were using their R&D results without paying them adequate compensation. Since the large part of the trade was being diverted to other countries some of them were facing uncomfortable balance of trade situation. In the light of these, they had mounted an active campaign at the international fora to have stricter controls on aspects of intellectual property rights. They had also brought about investigations and other guidelines relating to their exports particularly involving high technology products. Technological collaborations were guided to a great extent by the way the Intellectual Property Rights are accorded in the importing countries. They had also felt that in many cases their problems were aggravated due to lack of adequate protection and piracy in many of the developing countries. They had identified the necessity for adequate and effective protection of the intellectual property rights, effective enforcement of right as well as effective and expeditious settlement of dispute arising on such matters. These issues were introduced in Uruguay Round of multilateral trade negotiations.

GATT Accord

14. In the final Act embodying the results of the Uruguay Round of multilateral trade negotiations one of the annexures I(c) records the agreement

reached on Trade Related aspects of Intellectual Property Rights (TRIPs) including trade in counterfeit goods. In the Preamble, the text has recognised: that intellectual property rights are private rights; the underlining public policy objectives of national systems for the protection of the intellectual property including developmental and technological objectives; and the special needs of the least developed countries in order to enable them to create a sound and viable technological base. In this manner the importance of technology in development is interlinked to the Intellectual Property Rights.

15. The Agreement on TRIPs consists of seven parts and contain 73 articles. Part I contains eight articles covering General Provisions and Basic Principles. Part II deals with Standards Concerning the Availability, Scope and use of intellectual property rights and contains Articles 9 to 40. Articles 9 to 14 are on Copyrights, 15 to 21 on Trademarks, Articles 22-24 on Geographical indications, Articles 25 & 26 on Industrial Designs. Articles 27-34 on Patents, Articles 35-38 on Layout Designs of Integrated Circuits and Article 39 on Protection of Undisclosed Information. Part III deals with Enforcement of Intellectual Property Rights and contains Articles 41 to 60.

16. The scope of the intellectual property protection covers copyrights and related rights, trademarks, geographical indications, industrial designs, patents, layout designs of circuits and protection of undisclosed information. The scope thus is much wider than what is currently in force in the Indian Patent Act and other Acts in the intellectual property field.

17. The basic principles have elaborated provisions on national treatment, and most favoured nation treatment. Article 7 of objectives spells out that the protection and enforcement of intellectual property rights should contribute to the promotion of technological innovation and to the transfer and dissemination of technology, to the mutual advantage of producers and users of technological knowledge and in a manner conducive to the social and economic welfare and to a balance of rights and obligations.

Article 8 on principles has stated that a country may adopt measures necessary to protect public health and nutrition and to promote the public interests in sectors of vital importance to their socio-economic and technological developments in formulating or amending their national laws and regulations. This has also recognised that appropriate measures may be needed to prevent abuse of intellectual property rights by right holders or the resort to practices which unreasonably restrain trade or adversely affect the international transfer of technology.

18. Countries will accord to the national of other countries treatment no less favourable than that it accords to its own national with regard to the protection of intellectual property. With regard to the protection of intellectual property any advantage, favour, privilege or immunity granted by a State to

the nationals of any other countries shall be accorded immediately and unconditionally to the nationals of all other member countries.

19. Article 27 has dealt with patentable subject-matter as: patent shall be available for any inventions, whether products or processes, in all fields of technology provided they are new, involve an inventive step and are capable of industrial application; patent shall be available and patent rights enjoyable without discrimination as to the place of invention, the field of technology and whether products are imported or locally produced. It has recognised that the countries may exclude from patentability invention to protect public order or morality under certain circumstances. Similarly, exclusion from patentability include: (*a*) Diagnostic, therapeutic methods for the treatment of humans or animals (*b*) Plants and animals other than micro-organisms and essentially biological processes for the production of plants or animals other than non-biological and micro-biological processes. However, the countries shall provide for the protection of plant varieties either by patents or by an effective *sui generis* system or by a combination thereof.

20. Article 28 has spelt out the rights conferred and in particular the exclusive right of a patent holder. The patent owner shall have the rights to assign or transfer by succession, the patent and to conclude licensing and contracts. Article 29 has stipulated the condition on patent applications, in particular sufficient disclosure at the time of filing or at the priority date of the application, as well as information concerning foreign applications and grants. Article 30 has provided for limited exemptions to the rights conferred. Article 31 has set out the provisions to be respected when the use of the patent is to be allowed without the authorisation of the right holder. Article 32 relating to revocation and forfeiture provides an opportunity for judicial review. Article 33 has suggested the term of the protection for a patent shall not end before the expiry of a period of 20 years from the filing date.

21. Article 34 has outlined the principle relating to the burden of proof particularly relating process patents; briefly, the provision expects that new legislations shall provide, that any identical product when produced without the consent of the patent holder, shall in the absence of the proof to the contrary, be deemed to have been obtained by the patented process.

Future Course of Action

22. The final act embodying the Uruguay Round of multilateral trade negotiations was adopted on 15 December, 1993. By adopting the final act the participants had agreed to adopt the Ministerial declarations and decisions and to submit them for the considerations of the respective participant authorities with a view to seeking approvals of this agreement. Restricting to the observations on issues raised in TRIPs it appears that some specific

issues have to be addressed in this area. In the Indian context, current legislation on the subject are the Copyright Act, 1956, the Patent Act, 1970, the Trade and Merchandise Marks Act, 1958 and the Design Act, 1911. Amendments have been made to some of these Acts from time to time. Looking into the provisions specifically addressed in the area of patents, a closer look at the Indian Patent Act is considered necessary and some modification to the same will come about.

23. Some specific comments are offered on Areas of Patentability, Duration, Product/Process Patents, Compulsory Licensing, Licence of Right and use by Government and Non-Licensees.

(*i*) Areas of Patentability

The Indian Patent Act has excluded from patentability any processes for the medicinal, surgical, curative, prophylatic or other treatment of human beings or processes for a similar treatment of animals or plants to render them free of diseases or to increase their economic value. Similarly, inventions relating to atomic energy are not patentable. Substances intended for use or can be used as food or as medicine or in drug prepared or produced by chemical processes are also not patentable. The novelty criteria of the Indian Patent Act envisages world-wide search; this will need that any invention published before the date of the corresponding application of a patent will not qualify for the grant of the patent.

The Paris Convention had left the area patentable to be demarcated by the State. However, the patentable subject-matter under the TRIPs is relatively very wide and the exclusions are provided for in sub-sections 2 & 3 of Article 27. While there is freedom to exclude plants and animals, protection for micro organisms is necessary. Exclusions on the grounds of public order or morality is also permissible. It should also be pointed out that some of the exclusions envisaged is to be reviewed four years after the entry into force of agreement establishing the MTO.

(*ii*) Duration

The term of patent under Indian Patent Act is now normally 14 years. In case of inventions in the fields of drugs and medicines the term of patent protection is stipulated as 7 years from the date of filing or 5 years from the date of sealing whichever is shorter. It may be recalled that the Paris Convention has not stipulated the duration of patent and is one of the elements that are left to be dealt by the States. Article 33 of the TRIPs has specified that the term of patent protection shall be for a period of 20 years from the filing date. Here there are two issues. The normal duration of the patent which was 14 years will need to be enhanced to 20 years. Second, the distinction and the provision of the shorter duration in the areas of drugs and medicines would also have to be stretched to 20 years. The implications of a longer duration in the context of technological advances wherein many new technologies have relatively shorter span of useful life may not be very serious provided suitable care is taken at the time of entering into a technology transfer transaction. If this is not taken due note of it is likely that for relatively older technologies one may continue to make payments even after the real utility. In any case it should be prudent to relate such technology payments on the basis of actual production.

(*iii*) **Product/Process Patents**

Section 5 of Indian Patent Act has provided for grant of only process patents in certain categories of invention. It may be pointed out here that under the Indian Patent Act in all other areas product and process patent can be issued and have been issued. The Paris Convention has left this issue to be dealt with in the State's legislation in a manner of its own choice. Article 27 of the TRIPs has stipulated that patent shall be available for any invention, whether products or process in all fields of technology. In the light of this, the Indian Patent Act will need to be modified to be in conformity with Article 27 of the TRIPs. In addition, Article 28 on Rights Conferred has also to take clear note of the wide range of issues relating to process patents. Attention may also be drawn to Article 34 relating to the burden of proof following the grant of patent for a process.

(*iv*) **Compulsory Licences**

Sections 84, 85, 86, 87, 88, 89 and 90 of the Indian Patent Act covers various provisions relating to compulsory licence. Article 5(A) and sub-sections 1, 2, 3, and 4 of the Paris Convention deals with corresponding provisions. The TRIPs agreement has recognised the balance of rights and obligations. Though there is no specific mention of compulsory licencing, it appears that in view of the existing obligations of the States under rules of the Paris Convention provisions will exist for issue of compulsory licence in the domain of Patent Law in future. The Paris Convention has specific guidelines relating to the grant of compulsory licences. In the analysis that have been carried out earlier, on the provisions of compulsory licence in the Indian Patent Act as well as those under the Paris Convention it had been recognised that by and large these provisions are mutually consistent. However, it must be pointed out that Section 93(3) of the Indian Patent Act could make a compulsory licence in effect an exclusive licence. Paris Convention under Article 5A(4) demands that this licene should not be an exclusive licence. This may not still amount to incompatibility when such a licene is given under the Indian Patent Act in public interest or relating to abuses other than nonworking. It therefore appears that the issue relating to compulsory licene will not pose serious problem.

(v) **Licence of Right**

The broad provision of Licence of Right is outlined in Sections 88 & 89 of Indian Patent Act and in Paris Convention there is no direct reference to such an issue. While some previous studies had indicated that the provisions relating to Licence of Right would not be in conflict with the Paris Conventions, in the context of Article 31 of TRIP it appears that this will have to be re-examined.

(vi) **Use by Government and Non-Licencees**

Section 47 of the Indian Patent Act as well as Sections 99-103 deal with various situations in which the Government could use the patent for its own purpose. It also has specified that compensation or consideration are payable and wherever required to refer such disputes to the High Court. Paris Convention in many of these situations have left such issues to the State when implemented in public interest. Article 31 of the TRIPs has set out a wide range of conditions to be respected when the knowledge is used without authorisation from the patent holder. A very close examination is called for in dealing with the wide range of provisions listed in Article 31.

New Varieties of Protection

24. Several new varieties of protections are envisaged in the agreement on TRIPs. In the following paragraphs a few points have been examined.

(*a*) In the TRIPs, considerable emphasis have been laid on technological issues in Intellectual Property Rights. Explicitly protection for Layout Designs of integrated circuits have been provided for. Only very few countries in the world for the time being accord this protection. It will be necessary to provide such provisions in the Indian Patent Act.

(*b*) The rapid developments in bio-technology now calls for a wider range of issues to be covered under the intellectual property regime. Patents for animals created through human intervention and ingenuity is already protected in the United States. Many other developed countries are seriously examining this issue. In the TRIPs there is now freedom to provide or to exclude patenting of animals. This of course will be further reviewed in a few years.

(*c*) The protection to computer software has left a few questions as to which is the best form of protection. The Indian Copyright Act (Revision 1984) has provided for inclusion of computer software to be provided under the Copyright Act. In certain situations, it is felt that software which is already integrated in certain computer system, is to be protected differently; a relook of this may also be necessary, when the national legislation on certain aspects of the intellectual property are to be reviewed.

(*d*) The present Indian Patent Act has no provision to deal with protection of plant varieties. Protection to such varieties are available through certain other international conventions. The TRIPs has specified that the States shall provide for the protection of plant varieties either by patents or by an effective *sui generis* system or by any combinations thereof. This therefore is again an area which could be brought under a new Patent Act or by a suitable alternative system.

Concerns

25. During the last few years Indian industry have considered the issues under discussions at the GATT and expressed concerns on a wide range of issues. The most important among them being the one relating to: (*i*) Escalation of drug prices (*ii*) The right of the farmer to produce seed for his own use. Several Articles and clarification of the above has already appeared and these need not be repeated once again.

26. However, the question of the price of drugs wherever such prices increases are involved may be looked at from the overall cost of medical treatment in the country. Some of the high cost new drugs when compared with costs for other hospital services, may not be that large to become unbearable; more so if the hospital services to be provided at tertiary level are extended to patients coming from richer neighbouring countries.

27. Relating to the use of seeds by the farmer in the next season one should also examine the benefit of the new seed in terms of its higher yield, nutrition requirements and resistance to pests and diseases. It is quite possible that the second generation seed may not be able to reproduce all its full vitality it had during the first season. More research work, particularly at the grassroot level is called for to provide adequate guidelines in the use of cultivated seed produced by a farmer compared to the seeds produced primarily for sale of seeds by specialist agencies.

28. Another important concern is the need of the R&D system of the country to reorient its targets in terms of outputs which are patentable – in the sense there is novelty and has an industrial application. This will not only bring them closer to a domestic industry but also pave the way for successful transfer of technology from India to other countries. It is necessary to bear in mind that in the export drive of products and services patent protection in the country to which the products are exported is necessary to sustain the market as well as to protect one from disputes relating to patent infringements.

29. There are a wide range of issues in the agreement on TRIPs relating

to enforcement of Intellectual Property Rights. Administration of the patent office, effectiveness of other dispute resolving machinery, and the new linkages the patent office should evolve with them would also need review and amendments.

Conclusion

30. This paper has looked into a few points in the domain of patents in the broader area of intellectual property protection. The nexus of intellectual property protection with technology transfer and building of technology base has been explicitly brought out in the agreement on TRIPs. It is, therefore, necessary that during the time that is available from now on an integrated approach should be evolved in getting ready for the future, recognising that science and technology developments, industrial applications and intellectual property matters are closely intermeshed with the issues related to trade.

WORLD TRADE ORGANISATION[1] : HARBINGER OF A NEW WORLD ECONOMIC ORDER

PROF. NARAYAN DATT

Indian Institute of Foreign Trade, New Delhi

The Genesis

The Bretton Woods Conference[2] had decided to establish three international institutions, namely : (*i*) the International Bank for Reconstruction and Development (World Bank),[3] (*ii*) the International Monetary Fund[4] and (*iii*) the International Trade Organisation.[5] However, while the first two institutions came into existence on December 27, 1945, the International Trade Organisation could not be established. There was clash of interests. It was, therefore, decided to keep this proposal in abeyance. In its place a temporary body, named General Agreement on Tariffs and Trade (GATT) was established.

The Havana Charter

Based on the recommendations of the Bretton Woods Conference, 23 countries sent their representatives to attend a Conference which was held in Havana during 1947. This Conference drew up a blueprint called the 'Havana Charter'. The constitution of an International Trade Organisation was prepared. It was on par with the constitutions of IBRD and IMF. However, some significant countries, including the United States of America, refused to sign this charter.[6] As an alternative, it was decided to have general agreement on a

---

1. The original name suggested for this organisation during 1944-45 was 'International Trade Organisation'. During the course of the Uruguay Round of negotiations, the name suggested was 'Multilateral Trade Organisation'. The latest name suggested is 'World Trade Organisation'. The final name will emerge when the Governments of the Contracting Parties sign the 'Final Agreement' two months hence. However, for purposes of this Paper, we shall confine to the name World Trade Organisation.
2. This Conference was held during July, 1944.
3. The actual operations of IBRD began on June 25, 1946. The main objectives of IBRD are to facilitate investment of capital, to promote international trade and foreign investment and to supplement private investment by providing loans.
4. The actual operations of IMF started on March 1, 1947. The main aims of IMF are to promote international monetary cooperation, to promote exchange stability and to avoid competitive exchange depreciations.
5. WTO will be transformation of GATT, which was started in 1947. This transformation will take place on January 1, 1995. The status of WTO will be equal to that of IBRD and IMF.
6. It is interesting to note that while during the course of the First Round of Trade Negotiations the attitude of the United States was lukewarm, during the course of the Eighth Round, this super power emerged as a champion. This change of attribute is good for the world economy.

'contract'. And this 'contract' was given the name General Agreement on Tariffs and Trade'. Consequently the member countries were called the 'Contracting Parties'. GATT is based in Geneva, Switzerland. It is engaged in "calling for non-discriminatory treatment of trading partners and setting rules intended to counter protectionism and the 'law of the jungle' in international trade".

Eight Rounds of Negotiations

During the period 1947 to 1993 the Contracting Parties successfully concluded eight rounds of trade negotiations. The landmark round of trade negotiations was the eighth one, conducted during September, 1986 – December 15, 1993. This paper is meant to analyse the various stages of trade negotiations under the Eighth Round. Based on such an analysis, it is proposed to suggest a strategy for India so that there is no hitch to sign the Final Document during April 1994. In the meantime. We make a passing reference to the first seven rounds of trade negotiations. A summary of these seven rounds is given below:

First Round: The Havana Conference, held during 1947, was considered as the First Round of Trade Negotiations. The founding countries[7] exchanged tariff cuts for 45,000 products, worth US $ 10 billion of trade, on an annual basis.

Second Round: The Second Round was held in Annecy, France during 1949. By this time 10 more countries had joined GATT. During the course of these negotiations, customs duties were reduced for another 5,000 products.

Third Round: The Third Round of Negotiations took place in Torquay, United Kingdom during 1950-51. As many as 38 countries agreed for tariff reductions in respect of 8,700 products.

Fourth Round: The venue for the Fourth Round was Geneva. This Round took place during 1955-56. There was agreement to cut import duties further. The value of international trade covered by these cuts was more than US $ 2.5 billion.

Fifth Round: The Fifth Round of Negotiations was also held in Geneva. These negotiations were held during 1960-62. During the course of this Round, issues concerning the common external tariff of the European Community were

---

7. **The most significant countries which participated in the First Round of Negotiations included the followings:**

Australia	India	South Africa
Belgium	Luxembourg	Sri Lanka
Brazil	Myanmar	United Kingdom
Canada	Netherlands	United States
Cuba	New Zealand	Zimbabwe
Czeche & Slovak FT	Norway	
France	Pakistan	

discussed and negotiated. These discussions led to reduction in customs duties for thousands of products. The value of international trade eligible for cuts in duties was more than US $ 5 billion.

Sixth Round: This Round too was held in Geneva during 1964-67. This Round was called the 'Kennedy Round'. More than 50 nations engaged in international trade participated in these negotiations. It was agreed to cut import tariffs upto 50 per cent for a large number of industrial goods worth US $ 40 billion. A number of other agreements, including the ones on grains, chemical products and anti-dumping actions, were also signed by the Contracting Parties.

Seventh Round: Among all the Seven Rounds of Negotiations, the Seventh Round was the longest, toughest and most comprehensive Round. These negotiations started during 1973 in Tokyo. Hence, this Round was named as the 'Tokyo Round'. The negotiations were concluded during 1979 in Geneva. Around one hundred countries took part in these negotiations.

The Tokyo Round of Trade Negotiations included both tariff as also non-tariff measures in a comprehensive way. Even an improved legal framework for GATT was negotiated.[8]

This Round covered the following ten major issues, among others:

- Tariff Concessions
- Anti-dumping Practices
- Subsidies and Countervailing Measures
- Government Procurement
- Technical Barriers to Trade
- Customs Valuation
- Import Licensing
- Bovine Meat
- Dairy Products
- Civil Aircraft

Major Achievements of the Tokyo Round[9]

Tariff Measures: It was agreed to introduce a Harmonised Commodity Description and Coding System so that international trade is facilitated in terms of identification of the products. Consequently, all the contracting parties were required to transpose the schedules of tariff concessions into the new nomenclature. This new measure became effective on January 1, 1988. Waivers and permission

8. Since the Eighth Round of Trade Negotiations, named 'Uruguay Round', has brought about revolutionary changes in the international trade scenario, and which will be analysed in the subsequent paragraphs, it is essential to know the base of the new thinking. Undoubtedly, the Tokyo Round had provided such a base. Slightly more time and space is, therefore, being devoted on summarising the achievements of the Tokyo Round of Trade Negotiations.

9. Source: *GATT ACTIVITIES*, GATT Secretariat, Geneva.

to introduce the new system with effect from a later date were granted in genuine cases. Now, more than 90 per cent of international trade is covered by the HS nomenclature.

Anti-Dumping Practices: Already Article VI of GATT had provided that a country may impose anti-dumping duties to protect itself against dumped imports.[10] The Tokyo Round of Trade Negotiations gave a long overdue interpretation to this provision. The Contracting Parties were permitted to take anti-dumping action for providing protection to the domestic industry, provided all anti-dumping laws and rules of the concerned country were notified to the relevant GATT Committee and investigations were initiated and completed. The findings of such investigations should be to the satisfaction of the concerned GATT Committee. All anti-dumping laws can be reviewed by GATT on its own motion. The concerned parties can also approach GATT for conciliation wherever disputes arise. It has also been provided that consultations between and among the concerned parties may be facilitated under the auspices of GATT.

The anti-dumping actions may take different forms and shapes.[11] A large number of member countries have initiated a number of such actions. The number of anti-dumping investigations initiated by the Parties to the Agreement has been increasing year after year.

Subsidies and Countervailing Measures: The Subsidies Code[12] of the GATT provides a mechanism for international surveillance to ensure that the use of subsidies by a signatory does not cause any harm to the trading interests of others. In case it is proved that an exporter is getting undue advantage because of a domestic or export subsidy, a countervailing duty can be imposed by the importing country to neutralize any such advantage.

---

10. Products which are sold to an importer at a price lower than that charged by the producer in his domestic market attract anti-dumping duties.

11. For example, during the last few years, the United States took the following types of anti-dumping actions:
    (*a*) Definitive anti-dumping duties on imports of anti-friction bearings from Sweden;
    (*b*) Anti-circumvention enquiry regarding portable electric typewriters imported from Japan;
    (*c*) Initiation of anti-dumping investigation on circular welded steel pipes and tubes from Mexico;
    (*d*) Anti-dumping duties on flat panel displays from Japan;
    (*e*) Anti-dumping investigations on portable electric typewriters from Singapore;
    (*f*) Initiation of anti-dumping investigation of magnesium from Canada;
    (*g*) Initiation of anti-dumping of imports of nepheline syenite from Canada; and
    (*h*) Initiation of anti-circumvention enquiry regarding brass sheet and strip from Canada.

12. Articles VI, XVI and XXIII of the GATT constitute the Subsidies Code.

During the course of the Tokyo Round of Negotiations, the issues of subsidies and countervailing measures were discussed from different angles. It was made compulsory to notify the initiation and results of countervailing actions to the GATT Committee on Subsidies and Countervailing Measures. Emphasis was laid on conciliation proceedings.

Government Procurement: The Tokyo Round was responsible for the conclusion of an Agreement on Government Procurement. The Agreement sought to increase transparency in the laws, regulations, procedures and practices relating to government procurement. It contained detailed rules on the way in which tenders could be invited and awarded. The whole idea was to provide equal opportunity to domestic and foreign parties to compete. However, only a few countries signed this Agreement. Majorities had reservations and sought more time to sign and accept this Agreement. India was one of such countries.

Technical Barriers to Trade: It was agreed that procedures and systems relating to standards, testing and certification of products did not create unnecessary barriers to trade. Concrete shape was given to these initial agreements during the course of the Uruguay Round of Trade Negotiations.

Customs Valuation: "The Agreement on the implementation of Article VIII of the GATT, known as the Customs Valuation Code, sought to replace the many different national valuation systems in force at the time of the Tokyo Round with a set of straightforward rules which provide a fair, uniform and neutral system of valuation and preclude the use of arbitrary or fictitious values. The Agreement gave greater precision to the provisions on customs valuation already found in the GATT and has led to widespread harmonization of valuation systems along with much increased predictability in duties payable by traders."[13]

Import Licensing: There was an Agreement on Import Licensing. Its objective was to ensure that import licensing procedures did not in themselves restrict imports. It was agreed to use simple import licensing procedures and to administer them in a neutral and non-discriminatory way.

Bovine Meat and Dairy Products: In the field of agricultural products, the Tokyo Round of Trade Negotiations arrived at two significant Agreements, namely, the Arrangement Regarding Bovine Meat and the International Dairy Arrangement. Both these Agreements aimed at expansion and liberalization of world trade in meat, livestock and dairy products. Both the Agreements came into force on January 1, 1980. There are two international bodies to oversee these Arrangements. While the International Meat Council looks after the arrangement regarding Bovine Meat, the International Dairy Products Council oversees the International Dairy Arrangement.

Civil Aircraft: The Tokyo Round proved a 'boon' for the development and promotion of the civil aircraft industry. There was Agreement to eliminate

13. General Agreement on Tariffs and Trade, *GATT ACTIVITIES*, 1991, Geneva, p. 87.

import duties on civil aircraft and the bulk of aircraft parts. It may be pointed out that this Agreement helped only a few developed countries who were manufacturers of civil aircrafts.

Eighth Round: Wide-ranging international trade negotiations took place during the course of the Eighth Round. This Round started during September 1986 in Punta del Este, Uruguay. Hence, this last Round of Trade Negotiations has been given the name 'Uruguay Round'. More than seven years were taken to conclude this Round of Trade Negotiations. This historic Round was concluded in Geneva on December 15, 1993.

Main Objectives of the Uruguay Round

The main objectives of this Round of Trade Negotiations were the followings:

1. To seek further liberalisation and reduction of tariffs in respect of industrial products as also farm products;
2. To seek removal and/or reduction of quantitative restrictions and other non-tariff barriers;
3. To improve the mechanism for settlement of disputes;
4. To agree on comprehensive safeguards rule;
5. To identify Trade-related Investment Measures (TRIMs) which can restrict and distort trade and to suggest a time frame for their elimination;
6. To negotiate and finally agree on a multilateral framework of principles, rules and disciplines on Trade-related Intellectual Property Rights (TRIPs);
7. To consider and finally agree on a new institutional set up which will also encompass the GATT; and
8. To facilitate greater cooperation between GATT or its successor and other international agencies.

Plethora of Issues Discussed and Negotiated

During the course of the Uruguay Round of Trade Negotiations, while some old issues were reviewed by the Contracting Parties, a large number of new issues also came up for discussion and negotiation. Most significant of these issues are listed below:

(*i*) Conversion of the GATT into the World Trade Organisation (WTO);
(*ii*) Trade-related Investment Measures (TRIMs);
(*iii*) Trade-related Aspects of Intellectual Property Rights (TRIPs);
(*iv*) Tariff Barriers;
(*v*) Non-Tariff Barriers;
(*vi*) Rules of Origin;

(*vii*) Anti-dumping Measures;
(*viii*) Subsidies and Countervailing Measures;
(*ix*) Import Licensing;
(*x*) Preshipment Inspection;
(*xi*) Technical Barriers to Trade;
(*xii*) Customs Valuation;
(*xiii*) Government Procurement;
(*xiv*) Safeguards
(*xv*) Waivers;
(*xvi*) Concessions;
(*xvii*) State Trading;
(*xviii*) Customs Unions and Free-Trade Areas;
(*xix*) Balance-of-Payments Problems;
(*xx*) Agricultural Sector;
(*xxi*) Textiles and Clothing;
(*xxii*) Dispute Settlement; and
(*xxiii*) Trade in Services.

Harbinger of a New World Economic Order[14]

In our view the biggest achievement of the Uruguay Round of Trade Negotiations is the upgradation of the GATT to the position of the WORLD TRADE ORGANISATION (WTO). As was pointed out in the beginning of this Paper, the idea of such a world body had been mooted at the Bretton Woods Conference, which was held during July 1944. However, on account of opposition from some influential countries, particularly the United States, the whole idea was dropped as soon as it was raised. And in its place, a temporary organisation, christened as the General Agreement on Tariffs and Trade (GATT), was launched during 1947. The Agreement reached during the course of the Uruguay Round to upgrade and promote the GATT to the position of World Trade Organisation is indeed an epoch-making event. We consider this event as the HARBINGER OF A NEW WORLD ECONOMIC ORDER. This step will encourage greater transparency in national trade policy-making and will achieve greater coherence in global economic policy-making. It will now be possible to establish interlinkages between the proposed World Trade Organisation and the other international organisations, including the International Bank for Reconstruction and Development and the International Monetary Fund.

14. The title of this Paper "WORLD TRADE ORGANISATION : HARBINGER OF A NEW WORLD ECONOMIC ORDER" is intended to convey the message that this indeed was the biggest ACHIEVEMENT of these Trade Negotiations.

The World Trade Organisation will be headed by a Ministerial Conference. This Conference will be held at least once every two years. A General Council will be established to oversee the operation of the decisions of the Conference. Under the General Council there will be a large number of subsidiary councils including a Goods Council, a Services Council, a TRIPs Council, a Trade Policy Review Body, and a Dispute Settlement Body.

The main issues on which Agreements were reached and which will be implemented under the auspices of the World Trade Organisation are detailed in the following paragraphs.

Main Elements of the Final Act

The World's biggest trade deal was agreed upon on December 15, 1993 in Geneva. Acceptance of the "Final Act", containing the results of the Uruguay Round of Trade Negotiations was a victory of the negotiators of the Contracting Parties who had spent more than seven years on this gigantic task.[15] The 400-page Document will be formally signed by the Contracting Partics during April, 1994 in Marrakesh, Morocco. It will come into effect on January 1, 1995.

It may be poined out that agreement could not be reached on some of the issues listed in a previous paragraph. It was on account of the fact that disputes could not be resolved. Issues like entertainment, financial services, telecommunications and shipping were left out of the agreement or included in a stripped-down manner.[16]

In this Paper it is proposed to analyse the agreement in respect of the following six subjects only, since India is primarily concerned with these issues only and opposition in some quarters in India is confined to some of these issues:

1. Tariff Barriers
2. Anti-dumping Measures
3. Trade-related Aspects of Intellectual Property Rights (TRIPs)
4. Textiles and Clothing
5. Trade in Agricultural Products
6. Trade in Services.

---

15. According to Peter Sutherland, it was the most far-reaching trade agreement ever. He said: "I am convinced that today will be seen as a defining moment in modern economic and political history." Mr. Peter Sutherland is the current Director General of GATT and it was under his stedwardship that this agreement was signed. However, the "Final Draft Act", popularly known as the 'Dunkel Draft' was authored by Mr. Arthur Dunkel, the former Director General of GATT. Hence, credit goes to him as the prime mover of the Final Agreement.

16. Despite its flaws, the agreement is likely to funnel more than US $ 200 billion annually into the sluggish world economy by lowering import barriers as also by creating fairer trade standards.

Market Access

When the Uruguay Round started, the issues relating to *tariff barriers*, non-tariff barriers, natural-resource-based products and tropical products were taken up separately. However, at a later stage of the negotiations it was considered desirable to bring all these issues together. It was decided to club all these and allied issues under the broad head of 'Market Access'. The interlinkage between and among these various issues was, thus, clearly accepted. And the negotiations found it easier to analyse the various problems associated with market access.

There were many hindrances which came in the way of the negotiators. Even the negotiating procedures were not clear. Thought had to be given to the autonomous trade liberalisation process already undertaken by some developing countries. "The process was further complicated by the sectoral negotiations taking place among certain groups of countries. These negotiations aimed at reducing tariffs in particular sectors to zero ("zero-for-zero") or harmonizing them at low levels. And, while such efforts were largely being pursued by industrial countries, developing countries were pushing for a much greater commitment on tropical products."[17]

"The report of the market access group chairman, Mr. Germain Denis (Canada), submitted to the Trade Negotiations Committee in December, noted that some major trading partners expected to exceed the tariff reduction target (a cut of about one-third) with substantial reductions covering high tariffs, tariff peaks and tariff-escalation situations. He pointed to negotiations seeking the total elimination of tariffs on unprocessed tropical products and substantial reduction on semi-processed tropical products. He highlighted the important liberalization commitments being negotiated by many developing countries and more general efforts to eliminate or reduce non-tariff measures."[18]

Ultimately, it was agreed to cut tariffs on industrial and farm goods by an average of about 37 per cent. The United States and the European Community agreed to trim tariffs between them by one-half.

Anti-Dumping Measures

Negotiations on an 'Anti-Dumping Code' were started during the Kennedy Round (1964-67). The same issues were once again negotiated during the Tokyo Round (1973-79). But no agreement could be arrived at. The position remained the same during the course of the Uruguay Round. Nevertheless, during the course of the latest Round of Trade Negotiations a time schedule for introduction of such a code was seriously considered.

It may be pointed out that provisions relating to Anti-Dumping Practices

17. *GATT ACTIVITIES*, *op. cit.*, p. 22.

18. *Ibid.*

were already available under Article VI of the GATT. The only question for discussion and negotiation was with relation to implementation of the provisions of this GATT Article.

Once again the question of defining 'dumping' was taken up. After lengthy deliberations the term was defined. It was agreed that a dumped product was one whose export price was less than the comparable price for the like product when destined for consumption in the exporting country. Where there were no domestic sales of the like product, it laid down criteria for comparisons with exports to a third market or a constructed price based upon production costs *plus* other costs and profit in the country of origin.

It should be noted that any anti-dumping measure is a very sensitive issue. It is not easy to prove that a product has been dumped in the importing country. Detailed investigations are to be conducted. And during the course of such investigations all interested parties are to be given opportunities to present evidence.

It was decided that sanctions under the Anti-Dumping Code will be automatically scrapped after five years.

Trade-Related Aspects of Intellectual Property Rights (TRIPs)

Right from day one, during the course of the Uruguay Round of Trade Negotiations, the various issues concerning TRIPs have generated controversy after controversy. It has been alleged by certain groups that the agreement to toughen up protection on patents, copyrights, trade marks, etc., will help the developed countries at the cost of the developing ones.[19] Some other groups have, however, emphatically stated that such measures were long overdue.

What exactly the 'Final Act' provides in this regard? A set of rules and regulations have been prescribed, in keeping with international practices, in regard to the following 'INTELLECTUAL PROPERTIES':

(*a*) Patents;

(*b*) Trade Marks;

(*c*) Copyrights;

(*d*) Labels of Origin; and

(*e*) Rights of Performers and Producers of Sound Recordings.

We may examine the background. The question of TRIPs was taken seriously only during 1991-93. The negotiators recognised that widely varying standards in the protection and enforcement of intellectual property rights and the lack of a multilateral framework of principles, rules and disciplines dealing

19. A hue and cry has been raised in some quarters in India on this issue. We shall examine this and other issues under the heading '*Strategy for India*' in subsequent paragraphs.

with international trade in COUNTERFEIT goods had been a growing source of tension in international economic relations. It was agreed that rules and disciplines were essential to cope with these tensions.

The Uruguay Round Agreement, accordingly, sets out general provisions and basic principles, notably a national treatment commitment under which the nationals of other countries must be given treatment no less favourable than that accorded to a country's own nationals with regard to the protection of intellectual property. "It also contains a most-favoured-nation clause, a novelty in an international intellectual property agreement, under which any advantage a party gives to the nationals of another country must be extended immediately and unconditionally to the nationals of all other parties, even if such treatment is more favourable than that which it gives to its own nationals.[20] There is no 'umbrella rule' for all the intellectual property rights. Each intellectual property right has been treated separately. We examine some of them in the following paragraphs.

Copyrights: Contracting Parties are required to comply with the substantive provisions of the Berne Convention for the protection of literary and artistic works. Computer programme are to be protected as literary works. Copyrights of producers of sound recordings, producers of films, broadcasts of live performances, etc. will also be protected.

Trade Marks and Service Marks: "The agreement defines what types of signs must be eligible for protection as a trademark or service mark and what the minimum rights conferred on their owners must be. Marks that have become well-known in a particular country shall enjoy additional protection. In addition, the agreement lays down a number of obligations with regard to the use of trademarks and service marks, their term of protection, and their licensing or assignment. For example, requirements that foreign marks be used in conjunction with local marks would, as a general rule, be prohibited."[21]

Industrial Designs: Protection has been provided to industrial designs for a period of ten years.

Patents: Already the Paris Convention (1967) had made obligatory on the Contracting Parties to accept a set of rules relating to patents. Now, the Uruguay Round Agreement requires that 20-year patent protection be made available for almost all inventions in all fields of technology.

It has been provided that inventions may be excluded from patentability if their commercial exploitation is prohibited for reasons of public order or morality. Nevertheless, such permitted exclusions are meant for diagnostic, therapeutic and surgical methods. These are also meant for plants and animals (other than micro-organisms) and essentially biological processes for the

20. *GATT ACTIVITIES, op. cit.*, p. 22.

21. *GATT ACTIVITIES, Ibid.*

production of plants or animals (other than microbiological processes). Plant varieties, however, are to be protected either by patents or by a *sui generis* system.

Alignment of Domestic Laws

The member countries are required to provide procedures and remedies under their domestic laws to ensure that intellectual property rights can be effectively enforced.

Transition Period

It has been agreed to provide a one-year transition period for the developed countries to bring their legislation and practices into conformity with the Agreement. Developing countries have been given a transition period of five years. The transition period for the least-developed countries is eleven years. Developing countries which do not provide product patent protection in an area of technology have been permitted a period of ten years to introduce such protection.

Exclusive Marketing Rights

In our opinion, the Hon'ble Negotiators made an error in the case of the pharmaceutical sector and the agricultural chemical products sector. They have agreed that in the case of these two sectors the developing countries must accept the filing of patent applications from the beginning of the transitional period.[22] And this step has created avoidable problems in some of the developing countries. It is strongly recommended that at the time of formal acceptance of the Agreement, it may be provided that the transition period will be the same for all sectors.

It may be noted that the obligations in the Agreement apply to existing intellectual property rights as also to the new ones.

Textiles and Clothing

A number of developing countries, including India, were subjected to import quotas on textiles and clothing by the developed countries. In order to protect their domestic industry, the developed countries sought an arrangement, called the Multi-Fibre Arrangement (MFA) in 1974, outside the GATT provisions. It was a system of bilateral quotas. The developed countries which were importers of textiles and clothing and the developing countries which were

---

22. It has been provided that although the patent may not be granted until the end of the transition period, the novelty of the invention is preserved as on the date of filing the application. If authorization for the marketing of the relevant pharmaceutical or agricultural chemical product is obtained during the transitional period, the concerned developing country must offer an exclusive marketing right to the patent holder for five years, or until a product patent is formally granted, whichever is shorter.

exporters of these items had agreed to the import quota system as a purely temporary measure. There was every hope that the MFA would be discontinued and the trade in textiles and clothing would be integrated with the GATT system.

During the course of the Uruguay Round of Trade Negotiations, the concerned developing countries did put pressure for the discontinuation of the MFA. However, the developed countries were adamant in their approach. And ultimately it has been agreed to phase out the MFA over a period of ten years.

In our opinion, like in the case of patents, in this case also a formal agreement should be reached to abolish MFA with effect from January 1, 1995 and provide for a *transitional period* of 5-10 years to the concerned developed countries. The rules of the game should be the same for both the developed as also the developing countries.

Trade in Agricultural Products

Trade in Agricultural products has been brought under the purview of the GATT. The salient features of the Uruguay Round Agreement in this regard are:

(*a*) All non-tariff barriers like quotas will be converted into tariffs;

(*b*) Import tariffs are to be reduced by 36 per cent for developed countries and by 24 per cent for developing countries;

(*c*) The tariff cuts will be implemented over six years for developed countries and over 10 years for developing countries;

(*d*) Countries with closed farm markets will have to import at least 3 per cent of domestic consumption of the product. This share will rise to 5 per cent over six years.

(*e*) Japan will import 4 per cent of its rice, rising to 8 per cent in 1999;

(*f*) South Korea will import one per cent of its rice, rising to 2 per cent in 1999;

(*g*) Trade-distorting support for farmers will be cut by 20 per cent over six years for developed countries and by 13.3 per cent for developing countries;

(*h*) The value of direct export subsidies will be cut by 36 per cent over six years and volume-wise by 21 per cent. The base period in both cases is 1986-90, or 1991-92, if exports were higher in that year;

(*i*) The poorest nations are exempted from these farm reforms.

We suggest the following modifications in the above package of farm reforms:

(1) All developing countries which are facing Balance of Payments problems should be exempted from these sweeping reforms for a period of ten years or till they are able to overcome their Balance of Payments problems, whichever is earlier;

(2) The emphasis of 'compulsion' should be changed to 'opening up'. Let us illustrate. Suppose Japanese importers are not able to import 4 per cent of the country's rice, does it mean that the Japanese Government will place direct orders for rice import? This logic can be extended to other cases and to other countries. Hence, the Agreement should be properly worded.

(3) An attempt has been made to remove all non-tariff barriers and at the same to start reduction of import tariffs. This is a sweeping reform measure. It should be toned down.

(4) In case for purposes of domestic consumption a sovereign government extends support measures to its farming community as also to others sectors of the economy, why should there be international surveillance? This proposal should be dropped.

(5) When under the anti-dumping measures the importing countries have freedom to launch investigations against certain types of imports, why should the export subsidies be made a subject of discussion and negotiation? In our opinion, this proposal should also be dropped.

Although these recommendations have been made in the context of the farm reforms, they are applicable to all other sectors with equal force.

Trade in Services

Like in the case of Trade in Agricultural Products, the subject of Trade in Services was taken up for discussion during the course of the Uruguay Round of Trade Negotiations for the first time.

When in September 1986, GATT Ministerial Conference held in Punta del Este, Uruguay, declared that Trade in Services would be a subject of future Trade Negotiations, many of us in the developing countries were taken aback. A number of Seminars and Conferences were held in different parts of the developing world. In India, a large number of organisations organised such Seminars. On a directive issued by the Ministry of Commerce, Government of India, the Indian Institute of Foreign Trade had conducted two National Seminars. The first National Seminar on Trade in Services was held during 1986. A number of senior diplomats from the foreign Embassies and High Commissions based in India, apart from a cross-section of experts from the Government and the industry, had attended this Seminar. On November 7, 1987, another National Seminar on Indian Service Economy in the 21st Century and International Trade in Services was organised.[23]

The consensus of opinion then was that the subject of Trade in Services should be outside the scope of trade negotiations. The widespread feeling at that

23. This author had actively participated in both the National Seminars. In the Second Seminar he had presented a Paper.

time was that it was on account of the fierce competition between the United States and the European Community that this subject was being brought to the ambit of the GATT. This fear has come true. It was proposed during the course of the Uruguay Round to bring into the ambit of GATT services like financial services, insurance, tourism, telecommunications, entertainment, manpower, etc. However, on each one of these services there were disagreements between US and the European Community. And, hence, although the negotiations aimed at minimal market liberalisation, nothing concrete came out.

It is now proposed to continue these negotiations in future under the auspices of the World Trade Organisation. Since there are already a number of international organisations looking after individual services, like World Tourism Organisation, International Labour Organisation, World Health Organisation, International Monetary Fund, International Bank for Reconstruction and Development, etc. we suggest that the subject of Trade in Services should be excluded from the scope of any future negotiations of the World Trade Organisation.

Strategy for India

A strategy for the Indian negotiators would have been in order before the negotiations were concluded on December 15, 1993. And such a strategy would not have been different from a strategy for the developing countries, as a whole. Obviously, all negotiating teams had their own strategies. The negotiators did make sincere attempts to achieve as much as was possible. The fact, however, remains that these negotiations were primarily among the global players in the field of international trade. India's share in world trade is less than 0.5 per cent. The major players in this field are the following nations :[24]

Major International Traders	Share in world exports	Share in world imports
1. United States	12.0	13.9
2. Germany	11.4	10.7
3. Japan	8.9	6.5
4. France	6.1	6.4
5. United Kingdom	5.3	5.7
6. Italy	4.8	5.0
7. Netherlands	3.8	3.4
8. Canada	3.7	3.4
9. Belgium-Luxembourg	3.3	3.3
10. Hong Kong	2.8	2.7

24. Source : *GATT ACTIVITIES*, *op. cit.*, p. 6.
Shares in Percentages

The other countries which may have a big say in such negotiations include Russia, Taiwan, China, South Korea, Switzerland, Sweden, Saudi Arabia, Mexico, Austria, Australia, Denmark, Malaysia and Norway.

The fact, however, remains that India has a great potential to become a global player in all fields of activities, including international trade. India has vast resources in terms of natural resources, human resources, technical competence, managerial competence, political institutions, social institutions, etc. The 'opening up' of the Indian economy has already provided a base for the introduction of a large number of economic reforms.[25] The international community has, therefore, to take the viewpoint of India very seriously.

The Agreement on the Uruguay Round of Trade Negotiations has already been signed by all the contracting parties, including India. It is now a *fait accompli.* The Agreement has now to be formally accepted in a Ministerial Conference to be held during April 1994.

Right from day one when the Uruguay Round started, we have primarily been concerned with the following four issues:

1. Multi-Fibre Arrangement (MFA);
2. Patent System;
3. Agricultural Sector; and
4. Trade in Services

The major dimensions of these and other issues have been discussed in the foregoing paragraphs. We have also made a few significant recommendations at appropriate places.

The basic point which we should remember is that this is not the end of these discussions and negotiations. Under the auspices of the World Trade Organisation, which we consider as the harbinger of a new world economic order, all the agreements will be reviewed from time to time.

There have been views for and against this new emerging world economic order. As stated above, since these negotiations will be reviewed from time to time, we are inclined to side with those who welcome these new developments.

This Agreement will definitely help the world economy. This will also help the Indian economy. There will be manifold increase in our exports on account of removal of a large number of tariff and non-tariff barriers. The phasing out of the Milti-Fibre Arrangement at the end of ten years (although we would like its phasing out in a much lesser period) will definitely help India's exports. According to the Hon'ble Commerce Minister, Shri Pranab Mukherjee, "The

---

25. For an examination of the new economic scenario which has emerged in India, see, Narayan Datt, "New Industrial and Trade Policies of India" (Monograph, Indian Institute of Foreign Trade), September 1991; Narayan Datt, "Five Year Export-Import Policy of India" (Monograph, IIFT), April 1992 and April 1993.

Uruguay Round of GATT provided the environment and opportunities for a country like ours, rich in natural and human resources, to integrate itself with relative ease with the world economy."[26]

Almost similar opinions have been expressed by other significant leaders of India. We feel that those who are still opposing the Agreement are those persons who have a feeling of being sidelined, being neglected and being taken for a ride. Nothing will be lost in case such persons are also taken into confidence.

On account of the liberalisation of the Indian economy, most of the reforms agreed upon during the course of the latest Trade Round can be easily absorbed into the Indian economy. However, the Government of India should continue taking up its case with the WTO.

Specific Strategical Points

We strongly recommend that the Indian Team may take the following strategical points into consideration while accepting the Agreement formally:

1. More time should be sought for finally accepting those provisions of the Agreement on which there has been opposition in India. For example, provisions relating to the agricultural sector and patent measures. This course of action is permissible under the GATT rules.
2. India should reiterate the viewpoint of the developing countries that the subject of Trade in Services should remain out of the proposed World Trade Organisation.
3. It should be insisted upon that the transitional period should be the same for all sectors including the drugs and the pharmaceuticals sector.
4. The Multi-Fibre Arrangement should be abolished with effect from January 1, 1995. However, a transitional period of 5-10 years may be provided.
5. All developing countries which are facing Balance of Payments problems should be exempted from the agricultural reforms for a period of ten years.
6. The emphasis on 'compulsion' in various provisions of the Agreement should be changed to 'opening up'.
7. The reform measures agreed upon for the agricultural sector should be toned down.
8. Any support measure extended by the Government for the benefit of the domestic consumers should not be subjected to international surveillance.
9. Emphasis should be on anti-dumping measures rather than on the reduction of export subsidies.

---

26. Source: The Hon'ble Minister's speech at the Chartered Accountants' Association, Ahmedabad, January 23, 1994.

IMPACT OF THE URUGUAY ROUND AGREEMENT ON ASIA-PACIFIC ECONOMIES

DR. T.P. BHAT

Secretary, International Organisations Federation of Indian Chambers of Commerce and Industry and Indian National Committee of International Chambers of Commerce, New Delhi

Overview

From the standpoint of maintaining and strengthening the multilateral, free international trade system, it is very significant and highly appreciated that the Uruguay Round of Multilateral Trade Negotiations under the General Agreement on Tariffs and Trade have been successfully concluded amid prolonged recessions in most of major industrialized countries and amid mounting concern over growing protectionism or retrogressive, regionalistic movements in some parts of the world, including Europe and North America. The global trade agreement reached through the seven-year negotiations will serve as a new set of international rules on trade only in goods but also in services and on trade-related intellectual property rights. The Uruguay Round GATT accords are expected to lead to increased efforts of world nations to open their markets, further expansion of world trade and the revitalization of the world economy.

Although many uncertainties still remain as to specific economic effects of the Uruguay Round accords, the GATT Secretariat estimates that the accords will help expand world trade in goods by 12 per cent or $ 745 billion and global income by Rs. 230 billion (at 1992 value) in the next ten years. Reports by the OECD Secretariat and some other organizations also predict that the global accords will bring about a significant effect on the world economy as a whole.

A medium and long-term outlook indicates that it is very likely that rapidly growing Asian countries, particularly members of the Association of South East Asian Nations, will gain expanded trade opportunities in the years ahead mainly from measures by major industrialized democracies to slash tariffs on manufactured goods, tariffication of agricultural imports and discontinuance of the Multilateral Fibre Agreement.

Following are a few areas where Aian and Pacific countries can expect to gain as a result of the Uruguay Round :

Textiles and Apparel: A US $ 200-billion-a-year global industry, textiles and apparel are produced mostly in Asia, Latin America and to a lesser extent in Europe. The current Multifibre Arrangement (MFA), which has for 40 years governed a system of import quotas provided by industrial countries to developing countries, will be phased out over a ten-year period beginning July 1, 1995. Industrial country producers had sought a 15-year phaseout. The agreement calls for modest relaxation of quota restrictions in the earlier part of the ten-year transition, with most of the changes coming in the last five years. During the 10 years, tariffs on textile and apparel also will be progressively reduced – by 12 per cent on average in the United States. According to one study cited by the GATT, the value of exports of currently constrained suppliers of textiles and apparel to the US market would rise by 20.5 per cent for textiles and 36.5 per cent for clothing as a result of eliminating the MFA.

Market Access: Industrial country tariffs will be eliminated (a process called "zero-for-zero") on construction and agriculture equipment, medical equipment, steel beer, distilled spirits, pharmaceuticals, paper, toys and furniture. Tariff cuts on electronic products will range from 50 to 100 per cent on selected items. Tariff cuts on wood and certain non-ferrous metals are subject to further negotiation, which must be completed in the market access area for all products by March 31, 1994.

Agriculture: The agreement calls for reductions in export subsidies, internal supports, and market access barriers. Where imports had been banned, a country must allow imports a minimum 3 per cent initially of domestic consumption of the banned product, climbing to 5 per cent by the end of the six years. All quotas and other hidden barriers must be converted to tariffs and progressively reduced.

While the agricultural commitments must be phased in by industrial countries over six years, developing countries have ten years to do so. Also cuts in market access barriers are less for developing countries – 24 per cent on average for all products (no less than 10 per cent for each product category) rather than 36 per cent for industrial countries (with a minimum reduction of 15 per cent for each product category). In addition, the average tariff reduction on tropical products is expected to be around 40 per cent, though negotiations on specific commodities have not been completed.

Intellectual Property: When the Uruguay Round started in 1986, developing countries expressed considerable resistance to tougher intellectual property protection, particularly in the area of patents. At that time, they said that prices charged by industrial country companies in such areas as pharmaceuticals were unaffordable to most of their populace, which should not be denied access to such products. Industrial country companies argued that piracy of US goods was costing them thousands of millions of dollars annually and inhibited their ability to develop new products.

Over the last seven years, movement by both sides has been considerable. The agreement reached in the global trade accord is comprehensive, covering all forms of intellectual property, including strict limits on compulsory licensing of patented products by governments, often applied to pharmaceuticals in poor countries. However, the least developing countries have an extra 11 years to implement the accord and most other developing countries, such as India, have been given five years. Where there is no patent protection of any kind, in areas such as pharmaceuticals, developing countries have 10 years to put legislation into effect. Industrial-country pharmaceutical producers had wanted, but failed to get, protection for drugs already invented but not on the market.

What GATT Means for Asia

The success of the Uruguay Round of the GATT is viewed to be generally good news for Asian countries, although the picture, according to some reports, becomes more clouded on a sectoral and product basis.

Agriculture: In agriculture, Asian exporters of grains, beef, dairy products and sugar come out well from gains in world prices. However, by the same token importers of these products will suffer from those same higher prices.

The big losers in agriculture will be those countries which export crops such as coffee and tea, whose world price is under downward pressure. Rice exporters, such as Thailand, will both gain and lose. They will gain from access to the markets of Japan and South Korea, but lose as world prices come under downward pressure. The only obvious loser from the reforms of the Uruguay Round is Indonesia. The country will suffer losses in income caused by lower world prices for rice, cocoa and coffee, while at the same time facing higher import bill due to price increases for wheat, meat and dairy products.

Manufacturing: The biggest gains from the reforms in the manufacturing sector come from the incorporation of the Multi-Fibre Arrangement (MFA) into the GATT system. The planned phasing out of the MFA over ten years under the Uruguay Round offers opportunities for increased earnings to most countries of South and East Asia. This is true for economies as diverse as Hong Kong and Bangladesh.

Heavy manufacturing exporters such as South Korea will gain from the reduced tariffs in the OECD economies as well as from the reduction in non-tariff barriers such as voluntary export restraints (VERs) and quotas.

The position of China is complicated by the fact that it is not yet a member of the GATT system. While China will gain from the expected overall increase in world trade, it will not benefit from the increased market access opportunities negotiated under GATT. Overall, China will come out a net gainer from the Uruguay Round.

Services: Reforms in the service sector, negotiated under the General Agreement on Trade and Services, should benefit most of the countries of Asia, encouraging both increased exports of services as well as facilitating foreign direct investments in their own service sectors.

Commodity Prices: Boosted by the new treaty to free up world trade, commodity prices are likely to rise over the longer term, but most markets expect little short-term boost, analysts say. The most noticeable near-term effect was likely to be higher wheat prices as the US and the EC called a truce in their export subsidy war. A 5 to 10 per cent rise in real world agricultural prices is expected over five years, with the biggest gains in wheat. But this means poor developing nations will be paying more for their wheat imports. Analysts say that while grain prices are likely to rise as subsidies fall, the market will be influenced much more by crop quality, whether Russia becomes self-sufficient and whether China and India import more to feed their growing populations. Coffee, cocoa and sugar consumption might increase as the world economy expands, but the impact on sugar is muted by the lack of any specific commitment to reduce internal prices in the US and the EC, analysts add.

On Australia

Overall, the gains to the value of Australian agricultural production as a result of the Round are estimated to be moderate over the longer term. However, these gains are likely to have a substantial impact on net farm incomes. For major crops and livestock products used for food, the respective increases in the values of production and exports would be equivalent to 11 per cent and 13 per cent of the average values from 1988-89 to 1992-93.

In addition to agriculture, other Australian primary industries are expected to receive benefits from the Round. For coal, the European Union's program of reducing coal subsidies, already underway, has been formalized and reinforced by a bilateral agreement between Australia and the European Union, which was formally linked to the Uruguay Round outcome. This subsidy reduction program is estimated to produce benefits to Australia of between \$ A 300 million and \$ A 500 million a year by the year 2000. However, in contrast with production subsidies, tariffs on imported coal are generally low in the European Union and elsewhere, and their removal is not expected to lead a substantial increase in demand for imported coal.

For a number of non-ferrous metals, it has been agreed to reduce tariffs by a minimum of 22 per cent. For fish, some reducions in tariffs are expected in Japan and some ASEAN countries. These tariff reductions are expected to improve access for Australian exports.

As well as resulting in direct gains for Australia producers of agricultural products, minerals and energy, in terms of higher prices and greater trading opportunities than would otherwise occur, the agreement will provide stimulus to the world economy. Higher incomes associated with a more open trading environment will further increase demand for agricultural and resource products and other goods and services, including those from Australia.

On Republic China

Reports say that local industries are worried about increasing foreign competition in the domestic market after Taiwan joins GATT. Observers point out that the automobile, motorcycle, electric home appliance and steel industries as well as agriculture – which hitherto have received heavy government protection – would suffer the most from foreign competition.

The service sector will also face strong US competition following Taiwan's entry into GATT because American service firms have many advantages, including greater professional expertise and experience, analysts said.

Meanwhile, the government, with the assistance of CETRA, has designed a program aimed at helping local farmers cope with the effects of increased competition once Taiwan gains accession to GATT. CETRA has recently introduced the concept of Corporate Identity System (CIS) to the 305 farmers' associations islandwide to help them upgrade their management systems, become more self-sufficient and develop a positive and trustworthy image both in the local and international markets.

On Hong Kong

There are quantifiable as well as non-quantifiable achievements for Hong Kong in the GATT talks. For the quantifiable ones, the tariff reductions are estimated to be worth US $ 420 million per year on Hong Kong domestic exports. Electronic goods, scientific equipment, toys, etc., enjoy big cuts in tariffs, but there are no significant reductions for textiles and clothing. Nevertheless, tariff reductions in both domestic exports and re-exports is 1 to 4.

As to the non-quantifiable achievements, the Multifibre arrangement which governs textiles and garment quota will be phased out over 10 years, commencing on the date of implementation of the Uruguay Round, probably in mid-1995. As it is up to individual importer countries to choose which categories to begin with the release of quota, it tends to have quota relief for less hot items first, but hot items more gradually. Therefore, the benefits of releasing quota restraints will be less apparent in the first one or two years. Anyway, the artificial barrier imposed on the textile and clothing industries will be gone at the end of the 10-year period.

Analysts say that the phase-out of MFA will accelerate the restructuring of the textile and clothing industries, and adjustment in labor force. As the manufacturing workforce declines, production is gradually transferred outside the territory. Currently, only about 10% of the textile and clothing production has been moved out as it takes advantage of the Outward Processing Arrangement and at the same time observing the country of origin rules.

When quota restraints are eliminated, the textile and clothing industries can make the best use of foreign labor markets. As a result, only highly productive, cost-efficient operations will remain in Hong Kong. Therefore, the textile and clothing industries will stand in a similar competitive position as their counterparts in other industries such as in toys, footwear, etc.

Bringing trade in services, which account for 70-75% of Hong Kong's GDP, into the GATT will have three advantages. First, it means an open market for financial services, tourism, maritime transportation, communication, consultancy, and all other services. Second, all foreign service providers will be treated on an MFN basis. Third, all contracting parties agree to treat foreign service providers on the same basis as domestic service providers. In principle, service providers are free to penetrate overseas markets and export their skills and expertise. This will have the potential for big advantages for Hong Kong's industries.

Meanwhile, the agreement on the protection of intellectual property rights will benefit an increasing number of Hong Kong designers, composers and artists.

On India

The major trade and industry organizations welcomed the conclusion of the GATT Uruguay Round. Both Government and industry realize that access to global market is critically important to expand exports and encourage the inflow of foreign direct investment. The GATT accord supports efforts at sweeping economic reforms to obtain market access.

With the success of the GATT trade negotiations, India should be in a position to make better use of the market access accorded to a number of products and skilled personnel. The country is expected to increase her exports by US $ 2 billion per annum in the first two years after the implementation of tariff reductions. The reduction in export subsidies on farm products by developed countries will make Indian agricultural product exports more competitive in world market. On the whole, it is projected that exports of Indian agricultural products will benefit by an additional $ 850 million in the first three years and it may go up to $ 1.2 billion towards the end of the decade. The products likely to be benefited are: rice, wheat preparations, tobacco, fruits and vegetables, juice and juice concentrates, milk products, tropical products, etc.

The banning of safeguards and grey area measures such as voluntary export restraints and orderly marketing arrangements would help steel, steel products and leather product exports, in which India has distinctive potential advantages, to grow rapidly.

With regard to textiles and clothing, since there is no benefit in the first seven years, countries like India will have to wait for the full 10-year period before they can derive any significant gains, while tariff reduction will result in enhanced imports from competitors. In the transitional period, textile exporters will continue to face product quotas and ceilings.

Access to service personnel into markets of member countries will henceforth be possible on a non-discriminatory basis under a transparent and rule-based system. India can now open services sector on MFN basis as opposed to bilateral agreements. The gains from the GATT Round is estimated to be about $50 million in the first three years and will reach $1.4 billion towards the end of the decade. The services sector which will benefit from the agreement are : computer software, engineering services, medical and para medical, processing of insurance claims, legal services, films, legal and financial consultancy and banking.

In summary, the major areas of the GATT accord which are of immediate concern to India are : agriculture, textiles, TRIPs and services. In all these areas, India can look forward to some definite gains by way of exemptions from obligations and also by way of opportunities for greater exports. As far as TRIMs are concerned, many of the measures which have already been initiated in India are more or less in conformity with the GATT accord. Hence, the implication of the GATT accord is beneficial to India.

On Indonesia

Ginandjar Kartasasmita, Indonesia's minister for national planning, sees a special challenge to export-oriented businesses. "Our exports will increase, but we will also have to face imports", he says. "We shall have to compete domestically as well as internationally." Some see the GATT deal as additional incentive for Indonesia to dismantle its extensive system of protection for domestic-oriented industry – already under pressure from AFTA.

On Japan

GATT anti-dumping rules: Analysts say that new GATT rules in this area are a step forward for Japan, because they provide for restricting the overuse of such actions against countries suspected of exporting goods or parts at prices lower than domestic prices. However, government officials said they are still concerned about US reluctance to accept the stronger GATT rules.

Expanding market access: Japan offered an average cut of 61 per cent in tariffs on 6,800 industrial products, making the average tariff rate the world's lowest, at 1.5 per cent. It agreed to abolish, on a reciprocal basis, tariffs on pharmaceuticals, construction machinery, medical equipment, steel, furniture, agricultural machinery, beer, distilled spirits, paper and paper pulp.

Japan unilaterally removed tariffs on scientific devices, electronic products, film and some types of toys and rubber products. The nation played a major role in achieving considerable tariff reductions among major economies on scientific devices and electronic products. But it failed to get the nod for tariff cuts from the EC on household electrical appliances, where Japan and other Asian nations remain competitive.

In response to strong demands from the EC, Japan cut high tariffs on leather goods by 50 per cent. This will have a hard impact on the domestic industry, composed mostly of small businesses. The nation's non-ferrous metals sector also will be forced to speed up restructuring as tariffs on copper and zinc are largely reduced.

Opening up farm trade: Partial liberalization of the nation's heavily protected rice market is regarded as the most painful decision Japan took under the UR. In an attempt to get "special treatment" on rice under the GATT accords, Tokyo accepted tariffication on 22 farm products, including wheat and dairy goods such as butter and skimmed milk. In addition, Japan made a painful decision to agree to reduce tariffs on nearly 1,500 imported agricultural products, such as beef, oranges and ice cream. The tariff reduction is expected to push down domestic prices and negatively affect dairy farmers.

Because the beef industry has already been hurt by the complete liberalization of that market in 1991, dairy farmers – rather than rice growers – are likely to be the most adversely affected by the UR accords, some farm analysts predict.

Japanese policy-makers, farmers and agricultural organizations are going all-out to work out post-UR measures, which will likely be completed by April 12 when a ministerial meeting will convene for the adoption of its UR protocol. Most government officials and farming experts, however, predict no drastic change in the direction of the Japanese agricultural management.

Less textile protection: Japan's textile industry, which has been heavily damaged by an influx of cheap products from other Asian nations, is losing a tool to enlist the government to take protective measures against such imports.

On Republic of Korea

The Uruguay Round agreement is expected to have a positive effect on the Korean economy, which is highly dependent on foreign countries. Specifically, the agreement should result in a more efficient allocation of domestic resources.

As a result, the Korean economy's comparative advantages will be restructured and the decrease in resource allocation distortions will increase national growth potential.

Korea's export-driven growth during the last 30 years has been a result of importing raw materials, intermediate goods, foreign capital and technology, using skilled Korean labor to add value to those products and then exporting them. Although the agreement could negatively affect some sectors, it will encourage the Korean economy to grow more quickly through more efficient and more competitive production by expanding the factor markets such as labor, capital, intermediate goods, and raw materials, and through more exporting by further opening foreign markets.

The government admits that the Urguay Round accord will damage Korea's agriculture and services industries which have few comparative advantages in the world market. However, it estimates that gains from other areas will more than offset losses in the agriculture and services sectors. Merchandise exports will increase when tariffs are cut and such non-tariff barriers as anti-dumping charges and safeguards are lowered. Many projections indicate that Korea's exports of manufactured goods would surge as Korean exporters would gain more access to foreign markets following the Uruguay Round (UR) agreement. The Korea Development Institute (KDI), for instance, predicted that the new GATT accord would increase the country's exports by nearly US $ 5 billion annually. However, a report prepared by the Korean Small Business Institute (KSBI) on the impact of the UR agreement said that the envisioned phase-out of tariffs under the accord would result in boosting the price competitiveness of goods produced by Korean small businesses, but that would not necessarily bring about a rise in small firms' exports, given an international trend that non-price competitiveness such as quality, design and marketing strategy plays a more important role in expanding markets.

This projection is based on the fact that Korean small businesses lag behind their foreign rivals in non-price factors of competitiveness, which will be more crucial in winning a bigger chunk of foreign markets, the report added. On a long-term basis, however, it is still too early to make any judgement on the effect of the Uruguay Round pact on the future exports by small companies.

The report, meanwhile, forecasts that the domestic distribution market would be hardest hit by the market opening under the UR agreement. Local small construction firms and distributors would be overwhelmed by their foreign rivals who, armed with sophisticated marketing tactics and huge capital, would quickly invade domestic markets.

Meanwhile, the UR agreement on subsidies and countervailing duties is forcing Korea to review its industrial promotion system from a wider and more radical perspective. The main tenet of the agreement is that each government should refrain from providing direct support to specific industries or firms in order to boost exports or curtail imports. Analysts say that to respect this non-interventionist doctrine, Korea will have to abolish or amend many of its support programs for domestic traders and industrialists. This adaptation process will first affect the fate of many individual firms, especially small ones which have been the main beneficiary of support programs. In the long run, however, the process will also affect Korea's industrial structure as a whole as the impact will not be evenly distributed among industry. In this respect, the government will have to reformulate not only support measures for specific industries but the whole of its industrial policy.

On New Zealand

New Zealand has much to gain from the results of the GATT Uruguay Round. The most tangible benefits will be in the trade of agricultural and horticultural products but manufactured exports and the service sector will also gain from the outcome of the Round. Access to major markets such as European-Japan and the US will improve for a wide range of agricultural products, particularly meat and dairy products, as well as fish, kiwifruit and apples. The boost to agriculture is likely to affect property values, attract investment and stimulate more downstream processing of primary commodities.

The New Zealand Institute of Economic Research forecasts a 25 per cent rise in the value of dairy exports by 2001 and a 15 per cent rise in sheep meat and beef export values. Overall, New Zealand estimates a US$ 560 million boost to its exports as a result of the GATT accord, and a 1.7% annual increase in its Gross Domestic Product, or around $ 500 million on a $70 billion GDP.

On Pakistan

Pakistani trade officials said that the GATT deal would now make Pakistan's agricultural products more competitive. However, decision by Japan and South Korea to partly open their rice markets would help Pakistan rice exports only in the long run, they said.

Pakistan also hopes to steadily expand its textiles trade following the Uruguary Round's multilateral trade negotiations calling for the gradual lifting of restrictions on quotas within 10 years.

Pakistan's major source of foreign exchange is cotton and cotton cloth. The agreement is said to make it more difficult for importing countries to bring new textile items under quota restrictions.

On the Philippines

Philippine coconut and sugar farmers and traders said they expected the pact to boost exports over the medium term, but were wary about how the final rules would shape up. Coconuts and sugar are the Philippines' top export commodities, earning nearly US$ 1 billion in 1992. President Fidel Ramos said the new GATT accord would also offer opportunities for more exports of fish and fruits like bananas, mangoes and pineapples.

On Singapore

For Singapore, the completion of the Uruguay Round is a welcome outcome of events. It serves as the basis for an improved global economic environment. Overall, Singapore can expect a boost in the growth of domestic exports as well as entrepot trade. As trade in certain service areas will be introduced, the gain for Singapore will also be in its exports of services. In particular, the more rosy outlook for the US will have positive effects on the Singapore economy.

Conclusion

Current GATT obligations seeks to promote the complementarities of regional and multilateral trade objectives, but suffers three main defects:

- They allow significant sectorial exception (*e.g.*, agriculture);
- Overlook the distorting effects on trade and investment of voluntary export, anti-dumping and safeguards measures; and
- Allow the discriminatory enforcement of regional rules of origin.

In addition, GATT fails to track regional pacts after they are signed, when transition provisions or rules of changes can significantly affect market access for third country suppliers. The challenge is to close the loopholes in the trading groups to ensure that regional pacts do not compromise or undermine the commitment to the multilateral trading system.

There is a need to evolve comprehensive investment rules, including disciplines on the use of investment incentives and transfer pricing guidelines. In addition, there is need to promote the harmonization of national and regional competition policies so that broad predatory practices can be addressed at the source instead of through arbitratory anti-dumping proceedings. Therefore, it is necessary that procedures for anti-dumping investigation set by the new GATT agreement are followed in order to discourage discriminatory action.

International trade and monetary policies will need to be better synchronized to avoid pervese macro economic responses to macro economic distortions. There is a considerable challenge to establish better co-ordination between trade and monetary policies both within governments and between international organizations to prevent imbalances in macro economic policies from fueling pressures for trade protection.

With the results of the Uruguay Round, the international trade is expected to become fairer and freer, but it will continue to be fiercely competitive. Policy-makers will have to think ahead to ensure that they spot and adapt quickly to change in policies or marketing conditions in key areas. It is increasingly important for industries to think in terms of 21st Century market and press on improvements in quality controls, product development, market targeting, distribution and financing technology and so on. Increasingly, these will be the factors that will affect market share and profitability. The first priority in national strategies should be targeted towards building national competitiveness. The competitiveness of the whole system, not just the international competitiveness of products or individual firms, but with all the industrial structure and services of the governments. Countries in the region would follow industrialized countries standards of market opening, internationalization and liberalization.

There is a need to promote structural improvements in agricultural and services in Asia and Pacific. In the case of agriculture, governments have to come up with policies promoting productivity, compensate farmer's income and increase off-farm income. For services, governments will be able to promote the efficiency of financial and communication sectors by gradually opening them to the foreign competition.

Issues pertaining to environment and trade linkages, labour standard, social policies and human rights have come to the forefront in the post-Uruguay Round scenario. Unless these issues are tackled, they may act as a powerful constraint to global trade in the coming years. The Asia and Pacific economies must evolve and promote a balanced approach on trade and environment that takes full account of the development dimension. It is indeed necessary to check each county's trade, environment and sustainable development needs and priorities in a balanced and equitable way and it should remain focused firmly on trade and trade related aspects of the subjects which are within the competence of the multilateral trading system. In any event, environmental and labour standards should not be evolved to act as a deterrent to trade.

Recently, the relationship of labour standards is linked to trade and has been brought into sharp focus. The exports from low wage countries are alleged as "social dumping". This will act as a powerful obstacle to the development of poorer countries in Asia and elsewhere. Therefore, caution should be exercised in mixing social policies with the macro economic trade policies.

The impact of GATT new agreement on Asia and Pacific will be more clear after five to seven years from its implementation. At the outset, it appears that there are no outright winners or losers. Every country has conceded some grounds in order to obtain gains in other areas. This is true for Asia-Pacific countries and others. Expansion of global trade and greater market access is of high priority to Asia and Pacific economies. Now, their economic growth hinges critically on export growth.

THE URUGUAY ROUND OF MULTILATERAL NEGOTIATIONS OF GATT

K.R. GUPTA
M.A., Ph.D.

Introduction

The Uruguay Round of negotiations concluded by the 117 member countries of GATT in December 1993 were authenticated by their Ministers in the Ministerial Meeting held in Marrakesh (Morocco) during 12-15 April, 1994, paving the way for a multilateral regime governing the signatories' tariff, trade and related policies, rules and procedures beginning mid-1995. India is one of the 23 founding members of GATT which was established in 1947.

The Eighth round of multilateral negotiations, stretching over seven years of intense and contentious discussions covered fifteen areas including Tariff and Non-Tariff Measures, Tropical Products, Natural Resource-based Products, Textiles and Clothing, Agriculture, Trade Related Intellectual Property Rights (TRIPs), Trade Related Investment Measures (TRIMs) and Services, besides a Dispute Settlement Mechanism. Examined below are the important provisions of the GATT accord and their implications for India.

Tariff Reductions

The conclusion of every round of negotiations among the contracting parties of GATT since 1947 has led to progressive reduction of tariffs and diminishing of non-tariff barriers to trade among the member-countries. With the successful conclusion of the Uruguay Round, the developed countries are required to cut import duties on industrial goods by an average of 5% to 2.5% over the next 5 years, besides exempting about 40% of other goods, including items like steel, pharmaceuticals, paper, furniture etc. from import duty. These countries will bring down their tariffs, *inter alia*, on pharmaceuticals to zero, and on chemicals from an average of 20% to 6.5%. India's exports of bulk drugs and chemicals will consequently go up. Developed countries will also be reducing import tariff on agricultural goods, and this should benefit India's agricultural exports considerably. Enjoying MFN status, India is not required to reduce tariff to the extent that developed countries are obliged to.

India has made a tariff offer on industrial raw materials, components and capital goods, with the tariffs being bound at 40 per cent (where it was above forty per cent in 1993-94) and at 25 per cent (in other cases). Tariff reductions, where necessary, are to be carried out in six equated annual instalments from 1 January 1996. An exception will be the set of items related to textiles, where the period of reduction has been linked by India to the implementation of the textiles agreement (10 years, in phases of 3,4 and 3 years). As the reference date for reducing tariffs is 1 January 1990, when India's tariffs were very high, and substantial autonomous reductions have since been made by it, in the initial years India may not be obliged to undertake any significant tariff reductions.

Currently, just about 5 per cent of India's tariff lines are bound. After the Uruguay Round about 68 per cent of its tariff lines covering basically raw materials, components and capital goods, but excluding consumer goods, petroleum, fertilizers and some non-ferrous metals, will have been bound. In comparison, the principal developing countries in Asia and Latin America have expressed the intention of binding between 90-100 per cent of their tariff lines at levels comparable to, or lower than our bindings.

Preliminary assessment shows that reductions in tariffs by developed countries on products of export interest to India range from above 60 per cent (Japan), 23 per cent (EU) to 18 per cent (US).

Agreement on Textiles and Clothing

The agreement on Textiles and Clothing lays downs provisions to be applied during a transition period of 10 years for the integration of the textiles and clothing sector into the GATT. The salient features of this Agreement are :

1. All quantitative restrictions within the bilateral agreements maintained under article 4, of the Multifibre Arrangement, apart from other types of restrictions will be governed by the provisions of the Agreement. In other words, once this agreement comes into effect the bilateral agreements will cease to be in operation. However, the quota levels and growth rates incorporated in the bilateral agreements in force on the day the new Agreement becomes effective will form the foundation for the transitional arrangement.
2. The transition period of 10 years will be divided into three stages of 3 years, 4 years and 3 years.
3. At the end of the 10 year transition period, the textiles and clothing sector will stand integrated into GATT.
4. The integration of the textile and clothing sector into GATT would take place in phases as follows:
    (a) On the first day products which accounted for not less than 16% of the total volume of imports in 1990 of the products covered by the Agreement (listed in the Annexure) will be integrated by each Member.

(b) At the commencement of the second stage (at the beginning of 4th year) another 17% of the products will be integrated.

(c) At the commencement of the third stage (at the beginning of the eighth year) another 18% of the products will be integrated.

(d) At the end of the 10 year transition period, the remaining products (*i.e.* 49%) will stand integrated into GATT.

(e) At each stage of integration the products to be integrated shall encompass products from each of the following four groups – Tops and yarns; Fabrics; Made-up textile products and Clothing.

5. During the first stage of the agreement, the level of each restriction under MFA Bilateral Agreements (*i.e.* quota level) shall be increased annually by not less than the growth rate established for the respective restrictions, increased by 16% (*i.e.* a growth factor of 16% over the normal growth rate).

   a) For stage 2 the growth factor will be 25%.

   b) For stage 3 the growth factor will be 27%.

6. A specific transitional safeguard mechanism which could be applied to products not yet integrated into the GATT at any stage. Action under the safeguard mechanism could be taken against individual exporting countries if it were demonstrated by the importing country that overall imports of a product were entering the country in such increased quantities as to cause serious damage – or to threaten it – to the relevant domestic industry, and that there was a sharp and substantial increase of imports from the individual country concerned. Action under the safeguard mechanism could be taken either by mutual agreement, following consultations, or unilaterally but subject to review by the Textiles Monitoring Body. If taken, the level of restraints should be fixed at a level not lower than the actual level of exports or imports from the country concerned during the twelve month period ending two months before the month in which a request for consultation was made. Safeguard restraints could remain in place for up to three years without extension or until the product is removed from the scope of the agreement (that is integrated into the GATT), whichever comes first.

7. The Agreement includes provisions to cope with possible circumvention of commitments through transshipment, re-routing, false declaration concerning country or place of origin and falsification of official documents.

8. The Agreement also stipulates that, as part of the integration process, all members shall take such actions in the area of textiles and clothing as may be necessary to abide by GATT rules and disciplines so as to

improve market access, ensure the application of policies relating to fair and equitable trading conditions, and avoid discriminiation against imports when taking measures for general trade policy reasons.

9. A Textiles Monitoring Body (TMB) would be established to oversee the implementation of commitments and to conduct a major review before the end of each stage.

The Textiles Agreement included in the Final Act of the Uruguay Round envisages complete integration of the entire textile sector into multilateral framework at the end of the 10 year transition period. From India's perspective the most important positive aspect of this agreement is that it provides for dismantling of the discriminatory quota regime practised under the Multi Fibre Arrangement by some of the developed countries within a definite time frame. It may be mentioned in this context that international trade in textiles and clothing has been kept out of GATT for over 40 years now and that for the first time developed countries have come forward to agree to integrate textiles and clothing sector into the multilateral framework through a multilateral treaty.

During the transition period of 10 years, the agreement provides for slightly improved access for the products of exporting countries in the markets of importing countries through two routes : (i) route of integration, and (ii) route of growth factor.

The integration route provides that at the commencement of first, second and third stages of the transition period certain percentage of the products covered by the agreement will get integrated into GATT. This would mean that in respect of those products which get integrated quotas will disappear from the date of integration. While apparently this appears attractive, in reality, the benefit, especially from India's point of view is not likely to be very substantial. This is because the product coverage of the agreement includes products which are currently under restriction and also products which are not under restriction.

The route of growth factors no doubt provides for increased market access during the transition period which continue to be under quota. However, the increase in access one gets by the application of growth factors over the normal growth rates is not as substantial as India would have liked it to be.

The committment to integrate the textiles and clothing trade in the multilateral framework has been a major achievement. This is the first time that the importing countries have agreed to an unequivocal commitment to integrate the textiles trade into GATT. Article 9 of the Agreement provides that the Agreement and all restrictions under it shall stand terminated on the first day of the 121st month with the textiles and clothing sector fully integrated into GATT, and that there shall be no extension of the Agreement. The legal certainty of the integration has been further strengthened by the provision in the WTO text that any waiver from the obligations under an agreement involving a transition period can only be granted on the basis of consensus. That is to say, any member could block the consensus for such a waiver decision.

The transition period in the textiles agreement is balanced by the transition period in the agreement on intellectual property rights. Further, the transition period will enable India to devise policies and prepare its industry to obtain the greatest advantage from the integration of the textiles and clothing into GATT.

While the United States was insisting upon dismantling of the MFA arrangement over a period of fifteen years, India and other developing countries were able to get the period reduced to ten. In the concluding hours of the negotiations, the European Union (EU) and the US proposed that the benefits of increases in quotas under the Final Act should not be available to those countries which had not made a market access offer in textiles. The two were demanding both reduction in tariffs and lifting of quantitative restrictions on textiles products. This was a move directed specifically against India and Pakistan, under pressure from the domestic lobbies in the EU and the US. In intense negotiations, India stood its ground. A compromise was found whereby India agreed to augment its tariff offer by including in it 60 tariff lines covering specialized industrial fabrics etc. but not to lifting of quantitative restrictions. In addition it was decided to continue negotiations in textiles as the interests of some participants required the achievement of a larger and balanced package for these participants. In return, EU and US dropped their proposal.

We have linked our tariff reductions and binding in respect of textiles items to the implementation of the textile agreement. As an exception to the general rule of effecting tariff reduction in six equated annual instalments we have indicated that tariff cuts on textiles items would be made in tandem with the integration of textiles trade into the multilateral framework over ten years, and if there is any resiling by the industrialized countries, our tariffs would revert back to the 1990 levels.

Under the GATT agreement, India is committed to reducing the average tariff levels on 17 textile products from the current 85% to about 40% over a 10 year period. The items on which India has agreed to lower tariff fall into three categories: fabrics made from flex; special woven fabrics; felt and non-woven materials. After the phasing out of the MFA, it is expected that world exports of textiles will go up by $ 25 billion per year. At present, international trade in textiles is $ 240 billion a year. India's share in it is 2.2%.

Textiles and clothing account for nearly 30% of Indian exports. However, it should be borne in mind that elimination of the quota system will bring India face to face with stiff competition from China, Pakistan, Bangladesh, Sri Lanka, Vietnam and Indonesia. Our textile and clothing exporters have to prepare themselves to face the challenges which will be posed by a totally competitive environment.

Services

In the initial stages of negotiations, India had opposed that inclusion of trade in services in the Uruguay Round negotiations as it was apprehended that the results of the negotiations may require across the board opening of the services sector. As negotiations progressed the possibility of selectively opening up services sectors on the basis of negotiations emerged. The framework agreement – the General Agreement on Trade in Services (GATS) – has only two across the board requirements. The first is non-discrimination (that all countries will be treated on the Most Favoured Nation basis) and the second is transparency (that all relevant laws and regulations shall be published).

India had made an offer on various service sectors and sub-sectors which had been chosen largely on grounds of its own self interest, as it was felt that the entry of foreign service suppliers in these sectors would lead to spin-offs in technology, investment and employment. On insurance, the offer is limited to insurance of freight and re-insurance. On retail banking the offer is limited to a standstill and the commitment being undertaken is that not more than five licenses a year for foreign banks would be issued if the maximum share of assets both on and off balance sheets of foreign banks to the total assets both on and off balance sheet of the banking system falls below 15 per cent.

The US had made a proposal which would have permitted it, in effect, to make a two-tier offer on financial services. Full MFN treatment would have been reserved for countries making relatively large offers while others would get lesser benefits. This was unacceptable to most countries. As the matter could not be fully resolved during negotiations, a Ministerial decision has been proposed to the effect that initial lists of commitments would apply on an MFN basis when GATS enters into force, but at the end of six months after the entry into force members shall be free to improve, modify or withdraw all or part of their commitments in the financial services sector without offering any compensation. The implication of this decision is that negotiations on financial services may continue until six months after the entry into force of the UR results.

India's interest in the negotiations on services was primarily in the delivery of services through the modality of movement of natural persons. While Canada had made a significant offer, the offers of our other major trading partners (EU and US) left a lot to be desired. On the whole, it was left that the offers on movement of personnel could be improved. Accordingly, while agreeing to the Ministerial decision on financial services India proposed and obtained agreement that there would also be a Ministerial decision on establishing a negotiating group on further negotiations on movement of natural persons. The negotiating group will meet within one month of the decision, and conclude its negotiation by the end of six months after the entry into force of the agreement establishing the WTO.

Taking all relevant factors into account, India has limited its list of initial commitments in services by excluding from it professional services, certain value added telecommunication services, advertising services, some construction services and by placing a quantitiative restriction of 100 titles a year in respect of the audio-visual (motion picture and video tape distribution) services. These may be restored if there are improvements in the lists of commitments on movement of natural persons.

Agricultre

The GATT accord stipulates reduction or withdrawal of two types of subsidies: "Non-Product Specific" subsidies, and "Produce-Specific" subsidies. Non-produce specific subsidies cover inputs like fertilizers, water, seeds, pesticides, and agricultural credit etc. According to the final agreement, these subsidies have to be limited to 10% of the value of total agricultural production.

In the case of "product-specific" subsidies also, GATT calls for their limitation to 10% of the value of total agricultural production. In India only tobacco, sugarcane and groundnut oil are subsidised, and the level of subsidy given is also much below 10%. Besides, the minimum support price offered by Government for some 20 crops is also well below the international price. Incidentally, the GATT accord leaves out from the purview of subsidies any support extended to the small and marginal farmers (who constitute 40% of the land holding in the country) and also expenditure on infrastructure, irrigation, and electricity.

Even in the case of the 7 export subsidies which GATT calls for withdrawal or reduction, India is exempted because the subsidies given to agricultural exports are covered under Section 80-HHC of the Income Tax Act. Overall, one can say that if India so desires, it has the freedom to subsidise marketing, transportation, and freight for export of agricultural products as developing countries are free from any restrictions on such subsidies. On account of its unfavourable balance of payments position, India has also been exempted from the obligation to allow a certain percentage of imports of agricultural products for a period of 8 years from the date of commencement of the agreement. Otherwise, the GATT accord makes it mandatory for developed countries to give minimum market access to agricultural products from other members.

India stands to gain on account of the fact that farm subsidy levels are much higher in developed countries and they will be required to reduce them steeply. The reduction of subsidies by industrialised countries will raise the prices of agricultural commodities there. This will make our agricultural exports more competitive and enable our farmers to obtain more remunerative prices for their produce.

Public Distribution System

India has been successful in obtaining clarifications in the text concerning the operations of the public distribution system. The provision in the DFA was designed to rule out production subsidies in the garb of consumer subsidies. The language of the text, however, had caused certain misgivings with respect to its implications *vis-a-vis* the PDS. The clarifications obtained by India on governmental stockholding programmes for food security purposes and the provision of foodstuffs at subsidized prices for urban and rural poor in developing countries should set at rest such misgivings.

Trade Related Intellectual Property Rights (TRIPs)

The GATT accord covers 7 intellectual property rights: copy-right, trademarks, trade secrets, industrial designs, geographical appellations, integrated circuits and patenting. The important points of the GATT agreement in this area are :

– Patent protection will be for 20 years irrespective of whether the products or inventions are imported or indigenous.
– Animal and plant inventions, and bio-technological processes for their production are excluded from the purview of this accord. It does not require patenting of life.
– Except in circumstances which demand non-commercial public use of a patent by Government (where drugs have to be distributed in hospitals or public institutions), there will be strict limits on compulsory licensing of patented products by Government.
– Copyright will be protected for at least 50 years. It will cover computer programmes and data compilations. Authors of computer programmes and films will have exclusive rental rights, like performers and producers of sound recordings and broadcasting.
– Trademarks and geographical indications will be given stronger patent protection.
– Semi-conductor layout designs will have 10 years patent protection.
– Trade secrets will be protected from unauthorized dissemination.

Developing countries like India and Thailand have been given 5 years to implement this accord while industrial countries have been given 1 year to do so. Least developed countries like Bangladesh have been allowed an additional 11 years for implementing this accord.

For pharmaceuticals and agrochemicals, the GATT agreement allows developing countries 10 years to enact a legislation to provide patent protection. In the meanwhile, it requires them to allow filing of patents from the time this agreement comes into force in 1995. Since drugs generally require anywhere from 7 to 10 years for testing, new inventions will be protected around the time they come into the market, that is, from 2000 A.D.

India already has a Trade Marks and Copy Rights system of global standard. It is also signatory to the Berne Convention of Copy Rights. Out of seven areas (copyright, trade marks, trade secrets, industiral designs, intergrated circuits, geographical indications and patents) the problem relates only to product patent in food, drugs and chemicals. At present, Indian law provides only process patents. Under the Accord India has an additional five years transitional period. It has therefore to adopt norms and standards only after the agreement is signed, *i.e.*, by 2005. It is in India's own interest to have product patent regime.

The period of patent life varies from 15 years in Japan to 20 years in other developed countries. But in India it is only five to seven years in case of food, drugs, chemicals and fourteen years for others. The GATT accord provides a uniform period of twenty years for all sectors. Also, in case of process patents, the burden of proof in India is on the planitiff while the GATT text places it on the alleged infringer.

The TRIPs regime will apply only to patent applications filed after July 1, 1995. As it takes anywhere upto 10 years for a drug to enter the world market from the date the patent is applied for, Indian industry is free to produce and sell those drugs that are in the market, or will come into the market before 2005 A.D.

With the new patent regime in force, there is fear that drug prices will rise in India. But this fear appears exaggerated when it is noted that 85% of the drugs in the market will get released from their patents by the time the new patent regime commences. At present, out of 250 essential drugs (as listed by WHO), only 10 to 15 per cent are under patent. 28 major patented drugs constitute 80% of India's drug production. Of this, 22 will be off-patent by 2005. As such, only 6 drugs will be under patent by the time the GATT patent regime comes into force. It is expected that 6 to 8 new drugs will be coming into the market every year. These will be basically in the areas of AIDS, Cancer, heart diseases etc., and they will all be under patent protection. These drugs will be somewhat expensive, but the GATT accord gives Government enough allowance to get them produced under compulsory licensing in the country at reasonable terms and conditions. The Compulsory Licensing provision and the Drug Price Control mechanism can be utilised to protect public interest whenever the need arises.

The pipeline protection cluase (providing for exclusive marketing rights for 5 years for a new product patented in another country) will come into force 5 years before introduction of the product patent system.

Protection to Micro Organisation

Trade related intellectual property rights are proposed to be extended to agricultre. This provision is basically meant to provide protection to seeds of improved crop varieties in the form of what are known as plant breeders rights. The purpose of these rights is to reward the scientists and companies which make investment in evolving new varieties.

GATT subjects all laboratory developed and produced genes to international patents. Patenting is mandatory for all micro organisms if they have been developed or modified through innovative steps. However, the exact definition of a "new" gene or micro-organism, and the steps leading to their "invention" have not been defined in the final agreement. India will have to provide protection to plant varieties developed by investment of research resources through patents, or through "an effective *sui generis* system", or a combination of both. *Sui generis* implies a "system of your own", which means India will have to enact legislation to afford protection to such varieties. Naturally-occurring genes will not be patented. This is an endorsement of India's consistent stand that naturally occurring genes and gene sequences cannot be patented. Similarly, plants and animals are excluded from the Intellectual Property Rights regime. Indian farmers are free to use non-patented varieties, and retain the right to use seeds themselves as well as to exchange them.

According to the agreement, the Government has to enact a law for the protection of hybrid seeds, and for safeguarding the Plant Breeders' and Researchers' rights within a transition period of 5 years from the commencement of the accord in 1995. It is thus obligatory for India to set up a Plant Breeders Rights sytem for protection of plant varieties by the year 2000. Under the system, the Plant Breeder will have exclusive right to commercially market varieties of plants which satisfy the 4 basic criteria of an "invented variety": novelty, uniqueness, uniformity and stability. The Indian Plant Breeders Rights system will apply only to new varieties developed after 2000 A.D. Till the establishment of this system, all existing plant varieties that may be known, or are in use, will be in the public domain. In its Plant Breeders Rights Act, India can bestow upon the farmers the privilege of using their "farm-saved seeds" of a protected variety for growing subsequent crops on their own or leased lands, and also to exchange them among the village community. The farmer will, however, not be entitled to deal in such seeds and plants commercially. The PBR system will also give the researcher the right to use a patented variety of seed or plant to breed another variety without the need for any authorization from the original plant breeders.

India need not be afraid of the provisions in the GATT regime. It has probably the world's largest scientific programme in the field of seed improvement with twentysix state Agricultural Universities and more than forty ICAR institutes and research centres engaged in the work of evolving improved seeds. We have more to offer than most other countries by way of better quality seeds. In fact, seeds of our improved crop varieties have been in demand all over the world including some advanced countries. These rights should motivate our private sector to make larger investments in seed research so that the public sector institutions can utilise their limited resources for the development of our natural resources of land, soils and water.

Social Clause

The developed countries led by The United States have proposed a 'social clause' for incorporation in the new GATT regime. If the U.S. sponsored move to introduce social costing into the price mechanism for exports becomes a reality, developing countries like India will receive a severe setback in their exports. The U.S. proposes to levy a countervailing duty on imports from developing countries aimed at offsetting low labour costs here. In other words, the poor countries will be required to pay for the fact that they are poor. If the proposal gets accepted, foreign investments in developing countries like India would be discouraged because domestic manufacturers would not be able to export.

The American lobby is putting forward the plea that the aim of the social clause is to ensure proper standards of living for workers in developing countries. They fail to understand that the higher wages in developed countries are because of the higher productivity of labour resulting from superior technology, larger amount of capital and land per worker, economies of large-scale production etc. If developing countries try to pay comparable wages to their labour, the wage rates would be higher than the productivity of labour; in other words, labour would be paid more than what it produces leading to bankruptcy of the industry. The logic of advanced countries would lead the developing countries to the past colonial era when the underdeveloped countries were exporting agricultural commodities and minerals and importing manufactured products. The developed countries fail to understand the simple fact that in the world market if the comparative advantage of advanced countries for export of certain products arises from their superior technology and larger amount of capital, the same in less developed countries for the export of other products arises from their comparatively lower labour costs. If the developing countries behave in the same way, they can put forward the plea that the import of commodities produced with the help of superior technology and larger amount of capital per worker should not be permitted because that would harm our domestic industry producing with inferior technology and smaller amount of capital per worker. This type of situation, if permitted to develop, would lead to a substantial decline in world trade resulting in poverty for all nations.

To counteract U.S. pressure for Social Clause, India has raised immigration issue, especially of the technical personnel incluidng software engineers to the United States. As a result of strong opposition from India and other developing countries, social issues did not figure in the Marrakesh Declaration but they are being included as issues which would be debated at the preparatory committee (Prepcom) set up for creating the WTO. Apart from the linkage between labour standards and trade policy, other new issues to be taken up at the Prepcom level include linkage between trade and immigration policies, competition policies, finanacial services etc.

Environmental Protection

There is another proposal to introduce an environment protection clause. The purpose of this clause is to make developing countries pay for the alleged destruction of the environment. This is highly unreasonable on the part of the developed countries because it is they who are solely responsible for the damage done to ecology over the last two centuries. And now, the developing countries are being called upon to pay for the sins of the developed countries. The West wants to prevent Malaysia, for instance, from exporting timber to ensure that the world's forest cover is not reduced, but has nothing to say on compensating that country.

Institutional Structure

The Final Act of the Uruguay Round envisages the establishment of the World Trade Organisation (WTO). The WTO will have three main legal instruments : The General Agreement on Tariffs and Trade (GATT) along with the associated agreements and jurisprudence; the General Agreement on Trade in Services (GATS) and the agreement on Trade Related Intellectual Property Rights (TRIPs).

The highest decision-making body of the WTO will be the Ministerial Conference, which will meet at least once every two years, and will have the authority to take decision on all matters under any of the agreements covered by the WTO. During the intervals between the meetings of the Ministerial Conference, the General Council will conduct its functions, in addition to such functions as may be assigned to the General Councils by the various agreements. The General Council will also act as the Dispute Settlement Body. For the three main instruments, there will be three separate Councils, namely the Council for Trade in Services and the Council for TRIPs. These Councils will have the authority to establish subsidiary bodies as required. In addition, there will be Committees for overseeing the work under various agreements.

Assessment of GATT Accord

It has been estimated that the world trade would rise by additional $213 billion (in 1992 nrices) on an annual basis over the next 2-3 years period. These additional gains may go up to $ 450 billion per annum towards the end of the decade. The global trade on the whole may grow by about 9-10 per cent from 1995 onwards till the end of this decade. In other words, it is expected to grow to $ 7 trillion from the current value of $ 3.8 trillion. India's share in world trade is around 0.5 per cent. It is expected to gain from increase in world trade to the extent of $ 1.5 to $ 2 billion a year in the first two to three years of the impementation of GATT accord. These gains may rise to $ 4.5-5 billion towards the end of the decade.

It is projected that exports of Indian agricultural products will benefit by additional $ 850 million in the first three years and it may go up to $ 1.2 billion towards the end of the decade. The products likely to benefit include rice, wheat and wheat preparation, tobacco, fruits and vegetables, juice and juice concentrates, milk and milk products, tropical products etc. At present, India's textile exports constitute 2.5 per cent of world trade in textiles. The share is expected to rise to 7.2 per cent by the year 2000. Additional gains will be $ 400 million in the first phase of dismantling of the MFA. By the end of the decade (second phase of dismantling of MFA), the gains are expected to grow to $ 700 million. India's exports of services were $ 5.5 billion in 1992. Its share in world's export of services is 0.5 per cent and at present it is growing by 16 per cent per annum. It is estimated to grow by about 25 per cent from 1995. The gains from GATT accord would be about $ 400 million in the first 3 years and it will reach $1.4 billion towards the end of the decade. The services which will gain include computor software, engineering services, medical and para medical, processing of insurance claims, legal services, films, legal and financial consultancy and banking.

With the most favoured nation treatment, participation of foreign bank in the Indian market will be larger exposing Indian banks to intensive competition. To successfully face foreign competition, Indian banks must upgrade their efficiency to meet customer needs. The Government should also see that social obligations, particularly measures like priority lending, on nationalised banks should not exceed those imposed on foreign banks.

In the traditional period, textile exporters continue to face product quotas and ceilings. The developed countries should have been more liberal in reducing the rigidities of MFA.

As a result of introduction of product patents in the field of drugs and pharmaceuticals, prices of some drugs would rise by 30 to 40 per cent which would create some social problems. But there are alternatives from previous generations which will prohibit higher prices. Moreover India has the option of compulsory licensing or price control or using other provisions of GATT.

India has plans to make huge investment in research and development of drugs in the intervening ten years the country has to effect changes in Patents Acts. Union Commerce Minister, Pranab Mukherjee, has said that three to four bigh pharmaceutical laboratories might be built so that the country's qualified scientific community could come up with patentable formulations and products. Further the drug prices could be held in check through subsidies and by asking the manufacturing companies overseas to set up units here under compulsory manufacturing license.

Independent of obligations under GATT Accord, the Government of India has been following a policy of liberalisation and globilisation of the economy. This has been reflected in the budgets of the last three years. For instance import duties have been reduced from the peak of 110 per cent to 65 per cent. Foreign Exchange Regulation Act (FERA) has been diluted and the Rupee has been made convertible on current account. Foreign Institutional Investment in capital market is allowed. Many more steps have been taken to open up the Indian economy. The obligations under GATT accord are thus not inconsistent with the policies of the Government of India. The major trade and industry organisations have welcomed the GATT accord.

The emerging trade groupings, world over, are posing a serious threat to the growth of trade of countries outside the trade groupings. Since India is not a member of any trade grouping, it is always under the threat of marginalisation. The successful conclusion of The Uruguay Round averts this threat. Multilateralism provides much needed protection to countries like Indian who are not much important in world trade. The United States has been constantly threatening India to name it under Super 301. Strengthening of the multilateral system would reduce threats of such bilateral action. Super 301 is not only blatantly protectionist but also absolutely unilateral. It would be inconsistent with the new multilateral system. If India opts out of the multilateral system, it has to sign hundreds of bilateral agreements which is a very combersome process and the terms are sure to be far disadvantageous compared to those of the multilateral system.

In any multilateral agreement there has always to be some 'give and take'. Every country has to undertake some obligations to take benefit of the obligations taken by others. The consequences of staying out of the multilateral system would be simply disastrous for India. To take full benefit of its participation in the multilateral system, India should take vigorous measures to upgrade technology and modernise both industry and agriculture so as to increase its competitive strength in the world market. With its vast reserviour of highly qualified and competent technical personnel in all fields, India should be able to compete favourably in the world market. Technology is increasingly becoming the dominant factor in international competition. We should invest at least two per cent of the GDP on R&D in selective fields, particulary in new areas of technology such as bio-technology and informatics. Adequate attention should also be paid to the upgradation of our human resources in the technical field.

